The Wild Side
Weird Science

The Wild Side

Weird Science

Henry Billings
Melissa Billings

JAMESTOWN  PUBLISHERS

a division of NTC/CONTEMPORARY PUBLISHING GROUP
Lincolnwood, Illinois USA

ISBN 0–8092-9519-9

Published by Jamestown Publishers,
a division of NTC/Contemporary Publishing Group, Inc.
4255 West Touhy Avenue,
Lincolnwood (Chicago), Illinois 60712-1975, U.S.A.

00 01 02 03 04 VL 10 9 8 7 6 5 4 3 2 1

CONTENTS

UNIT THREE

To the Student

Astronomy, biology, psychology, physics, chemistry—for many people, studying science is a way of discovering new frontiers. That is because technology and research have allowed scientists to uncover new facts about living organisms, Earth, and worlds beyond. The articles in *Weird Science* go deep into the mysteries of science—some that are still in the early stages of discovery. These articles focus on details of natural healing, time travel, supernatural experiences, and other subjects of scientific investigation that fascinate even as they shock, repel, or mystify. After becoming aware of such amazing happenings and fantastic theories, no reader can hold on to the attitude that science is only for specialists.

As you read and enjoy the 15 articles in this book, you will be developing your reading skills. If you complete all the lessons in this book, you will surely increase your reading speed and improve your reading comprehension and critical thinking skills. Also, because these exercises include items of the types often found on state and national tests, learning how to complete them will prepare you for tests you may have to take in the future.

How to Use This Book

About the Book.   *Weird Science* contains three units, each of which includes five lessons. Each lesson begins with an article about an unusual subject or event. The article is followed by a group of four reading comprehension exercises and three critical thinking exercises. The reading comprehension exercises will help you understand the article. The critical thinking exercises will help you think about what you have read and how it relates to your own experience.

At the end of each lesson, you will also have the opportunity to give your personal response to some aspect of the article and then to assess how well you understood what you read.

The Sample Lesson.   Working through the sample lesson, the first lesson in the book, with your class or group will demonstrate how a lesson is organized. The sample lesson explains how to complete the exercises and score your answers. The correct answers for the sample exercises and sample scores are printed in lighter type. In some cases, explanations of the correct answers are given. The explanations will help you understand how to think through these question types.

If you have any questions about how to complete the exercises or score them, this is the time to get the answers.

Working Through Each Lesson.   Begin each lesson by looking at the photograph and reading the caption. Before you read, predict what you think the article will be about. Then read the article.

Sometimes your teacher may decide to time your reading. Timing helps you keep track of and increase your reading speed. If you have been timed, enter your reading time in the box at the end of the lesson. Then use the Words-per-Minute Table to find your reading speed, and record your speed on the Reading Speed graph at the end of the unit.

Next complete the Reading Comprehension and Critical Thinking exercises. The directions for each exercise will tell you how to mark your answers. When you have finished all four Reading Comprehension exercises, use the answer key provided by your teacher to check your work. Follow the directions after each exercise to find your score. Record your Reading Comprehension scores on the graph at the end of each unit. Then check your answers to the Author's Approach, Summarizing and Paraphrasing, and Critical Thinking exercises. Fill in the Critical Thinking Chart at the end of each unit with your evaluation of your work and comments about your progress.

At the end of each unit you will also complete a Compare and Contrast Chart. The completed chart will help you see what the articles have in common, and it will give you an opportunity to explore your own ideas about the events in the articles.

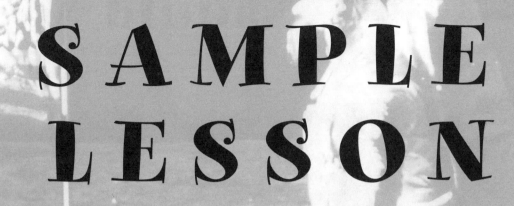

SAMPLE
LESSON

Should We Blow Up the Moon?

Most people like the moon just the way it is. They write poems about it. They sing love songs to it. They hold hands under it. But Alexander Abian has a scheme that would change all that. He wants to blow up the moon!

2   Abian is a mathematics professor at Iowa State University. He has a bold plan. First he wants to send some astronauts to the moon. They would drill a huge hole in the moon's surface. Into this hole they would tuck some nuclear bombs. After the astronauts are safely out of the way, someone back on Earth would push a remote control button. One second later, the moon would be blown to bits.

3   Why does Abian want to do this? He thinks it would improve the earth's weather. With the moon out of the way, he says, there would be no more blizzards in the Rocky Mountains. There would be no killer typhoons in Asia. Summer heat waves in New York City would end. So, too, would droughts in Africa. Not only would bad things end, but good things would start. According to Abian, the deserts and arctic regions would bloom. After we blow up the moon, says the professor, we would have pleasant weather all year long.

4   What does the moon have to do with snowstorms in Denver or floods in Bangladesh? Plenty, says Abian. The moon's gravity pulls on the earth. That tug keeps the earth tilted at a $23\frac{1}{2}$-degree angle. And that's the problem. It is this tilt that gives us our seasons. The side of the earth tilted toward the sun has summer and sweltering weather. The side tilted away from the sun has winter and chilling cold.

5   Now suppose we blow up the moon. According to Abian, the earth would then lose its $23\frac{1}{2}$-degree tilt. The amount of sunlight would no longer change with the seasons. It would be the same all year long. "Perpetual spring!" promises Abian.

6   So why haven't we blown up the moon? Most people like having it around. More than a dozen countries like it so much they have put it on their national flags. Abian understands that. So he has come up with a second plan. He says we could try having two moons. We could "bring a moon from Mars." It could be put on the other side of Earth from the first moon. That way, its pull would balance off the pull of the original moon. Now the Earth would have two moons but no tilt!

7   There is another serious problem with blowing up the moon. True, it might get rid of the earth's tilt. But such a change might cause massive earthquakes. David Taylor of Northwestern University observes, "[Abian] would destroy civilization.

Buzz Aldrin stands next to the American flag that the Apollo 11 landing crew placed on the moon in July 1969. If you're set on visiting the moon, perhaps you'd better hurry. If Professor Alexander Abian has his way, the moon won't be around much longer.

But we'd have great weather." Thomas Stix of Princeton adds that most scientists wouldn't touch Abian's idea "with a 10-foot pole."

8 Such talk doesn't bother Abian. He wants to shake things up. Why, he asks, do we have to accept the solar system the way it is? Why can't we move things around? Abian has some other ideas as well. He would like to change the orbit of Venus. It's too close to the sun, he says. Temperatures on Venus are a toasty 900°F. Abian thinks we should move Venus away from the sun. That would cool the planet and perhaps make it fit for human life. How does Abian recommend we move Venus? "We can shoot it with rockets," he suggests.

9 No one is holding his or her breath waiting for these things to happen. Even Abian knows that other scientists think his ideas are a bit strange. "I don't think [anything will happen] in my lifetime or in my children's lifetime," he says. "But I want to plant the seed."

If you have been timed while reading this article, enter your reading time below. Then turn to the Words-per-Minute Table on page 55 and look up your reading speed (words per minute). Enter your reading speed on the graph on page 56.

Reading Time: Sample Lesson

———— : ————

Minutes　　*Seconds*

A | Finding the Main Idea

One statement below expresses the main idea of the article. One statement is too general, or too broad. The other statement explains only part of the article; it is too narrow. Label the statements using the following key:

M—Main Idea   **B—Too Broad**   **N—Too Narrow**

___N___ 1. Professors at Northwestern University and at Princeton disagree with the ideas of Alexander Abian. [This statement is true, but it is *too narrow*. It doesn't suggest what Abian's ideas are about.]

___M___ 2. Mathematics professor Alexander Abian has proposed blowing up the moon as a way of improving weather on Earth. [This is the *main idea*. It tells whom the article is about and what he did.]

___B___ 3. It's hard to tell whether some theories about the universe should be taken seriously. [This statement is *too broad*. It doesn't tell which theory the article is about.]

___15___ Score 15 points for a correct M answer.

___10___ Score 5 points for each correct B or N answer.

___25___ **Total Score:** Finding the Main Idea

B | Recalling Facts

How well do you remember the facts in the article? Put an X in the box next to the answer that correctly completes each statement about the article.

1. Abian's theory is that destroying the moon will
   ☐ a. cause Earth to tilt at a 23½-degree angle.
   ☐ b. cause massive earthquakes.
   ☒ c. improve weather on Earth.

2. The side of Earth tilted toward the sun has
   ☒ a. summer.
   ☐ b. winter.
   ☐ c. perpetual spring.

3. Abian also suggests moving
   ☐ a. the moon to a new orbit.
   ☐ b. Earth closer to Venus.
   ☒ c. a moon from Mars to orbit Earth.

4. One way to move Venus, Abian says, is to
   ☒ a. shoot it with rockets.
   ☐ b. set off nuclear bombs on it.
   ☐ c. use a 10-foot pole as a lever.

5. Abian expects his ideas to get serious attention
   ☐ a next year.
   ☐ b. during his lifetime.
   ☒ c. in the distant future.

Score 5 points for each correct answer.

___25___ **Total Score:** Recalling Facts

C | Making Inferences

When you combine your own experience and information from a text to draw a conclusion that is not directly stated in that text, you are making an inference. Below are five statements that may or may not be inferences based on information in the article. Label the statements using the following key:

C—Correct Inference   **F—Faulty Inference**

___F___ 1. Most mathematics professors are more creative than scientists. [This is a faulty inference. It makes a value judgment without supporting evidence.]

___F___ 2. Other professors criticize Professor Abian's ideas because they are jealous of him. [This is a faulty inference. Other reasons are given.]

___C___ 3. As we humans gain power over nature, we must guard against unwise use of this power. [This is a correct inference. Abian suggests using present technology to make vast changes.]

___C___ 4. Humans cannot live on or even explore Venus. [This is a correct inference. The temperature of Venus is 900°F.]

___C___ 5. Professor Abian's main goal in proposing "corrections" to the universe is to get people to take a fresh look at things they take for granted. [This is a correct inference. Abian says, "I want to plant the seed."]

> Score 5 points for each correct answer.
>
> ___25___ **Total Score:** Making Inferences

D | Using Words Precisely

Each numbered sentence below contains an underlined word or phrase from the article. Following the sentence are three definitions. One definition is closest to the meaning of the underlined word. One definition is opposite or nearly opposite. Label those two definitions using the following key; do not label the remaining definition.

C—Closest   **O—Opposite or Nearly Opposite**

1. After the astronauts are safely out of the way, someone back on Earth would push a <u>remote</u> control button.

___C___ a. distant

___O___ b. close

_____ c. powerful

2. Summer heat waves in New York City would end. So, too, would <u>droughts</u> in Africa.

___O___ a. floods

_____ b. sicknesses

___C___ c. unusually dry spells

3. The side of Earth tilted toward the sun has summer and <u>sweltering</u> weather.

___C___ a. extremely hot and humid

___O___ b. very cold

_____ c. cloudy

4. "<u>Perpetual</u> spring!" promises Abian.

_____ a. dangerous

___O___ b. temporary

___C___ c. everlasting

5. How does Abian <u>recommend</u> we move Venus?

_____C_____ a. advise that

_____ b. recall that

_____O_____ c. discredit the idea that

_____15_____	Score 3 points for each correct C answer.
_____10_____	Score 2 points for each correct O answer.
_____25_____	**Total Score:** Using Words Precisely

Enter the four total scores in the spaces below, and add them together to find your Reading Comprehension Score. Then record your score on the graph on page 57.

Score	Question Type	Sample Lesson
_____25_____	Finding the Main Idea	
_____25_____	Recalling Facts	
_____25_____	Making Inferences	
_____25_____	Using Words Precisely	
_____100_____	**Reading Comprehension Score**	

Author's Approach

Put an X in the box next to the correct answer.

1. The main purpose of the first paragraph is to

☒ a. contrast Alexander Abian's plan for the moon with most people's ideas about the moon.

☐ b. explain how and why Alexander Abian wants to blow up the moon.

☐ c. stress how much most people like the moon.

2. From the statements below, choose those that you believe the authors would agree with.

☒ a. Most people think that Professor Abian's plan is ridiculous.

☐ b. Professor Abian is an original thinker.

☐ c. Professor Abian's plan will probably be carried out someday.

3. What do the authors imply by saying "David Taylor of Northwestern University observes, '[Abian] would destroy civilization. But we'd have great weather'"?

☐ a. David Taylor thinks that good weather is more important than civilization.

☒ b. David Taylor is opposed to Abian's plan.

☐ c. David Taylor agrees with Abian's plan.

4. The authors probably wrote this article to

☐ a. persuade readers to support Abian's plans.

☐ b. encourage readers to respect those who think differently from them.

☒ c. inform readers of an extreme suggestion for the moon.

_____4_____	Number of correct answers

Record your personal assessment of your work on the Critical Thinking Chart on page 58.

Summarizing and Paraphrasing

Put an X in the box next to the correct answer.

1. Below are summaries of the article. Choose the summary that says all the most important things about the article but in the fewest words.

☐ a. Alexander Abian thinks we should blow up the moon.
   [This summary leaves out almost all of the important details, such as who Abian is and why he believes we should destroy the moon.]

☐ b. Alexander Abian believes that we should blow up the moon. If the moon were destroyed, this mathematics professor at Iowa State University says, the earth would no longer be tilted at a 23 $\frac{1}{2}$-degree angle. If Earth weren't tilted, the amount of sunlight striking every part of the planet would stay the same all year. Weather would improve all over the world. [This summary presents many important ideas from the article but includes too many unnecessary details.]

☒ c. Mathematics professor Alexander Abian believes that if the moon were destroyed, Earth would no longer experience seasons, and weather would improve. He also has other ideas about how to change the solar system. Abian's ideas are not widely accepted by other scientists. [This summary says all the most important things about the article in the fewest words.]

2. Read the statement from the article below. Then read the paraphrase of that statement. Choose the reason that best tells why the paraphrase does not say the same thing as the statement.

   Statement: Since Abian's goal is to straighten out the earth, he has suggested that we bring in a moon from Mars to balance out the pull from our own moon.

   Paraphrase: Because Abian wants to get rid of the earth's tilt, he has made another interesting suggestion involving Mars and its moon.

☐ a. Paraphrase says too much.

☒ b. Paraphrase doesn't say enough. [This statement fails to explain Abian's plan for Mars and its moon.]

☐ c. Paraphrase doesn't agree with the statement.

> _____2_____ Number of correct answers
>
> Record your personal assessment of your work on the Critical Thinking Chart on page 58.

Critical Thinking

Follow the directions provided for questions 1, 2, and 3. Put an X in the box next to the correct answer for the other questions.

1. For each statement below, write _O_ if it expresses an opinion or write _F_ if it expresses a fact.

   __O__ a. Professor Abian is one of the finest thinkers of our time.

   __F__ b. The earth's tilt causes the seasons.

   __F__ c. The temperature on Venus can reach 900°F.

2. Choose from the letters below to correctly complete the following statement. Write the letters on the lines.

   On the positive side, __b__, but on the negative side __a__.

   a. destroying the moon could cause earthquakes

   b. people on Earth would have less extreme weather if the moon were destroyed

   c. blowing up the moon is an unusual idea

3. Choose from the letters below to correctly complete the following statement. Write the letters on the lines.

According to Abian, ___c___ would cause Earth to ___a___, and the effect would be ___b___.

a. lose its tilt

b. no more seasons

c. destroying the moon

4. Of the following theme categories, which would this story fit into?

☒ a. Don't be afraid to think original thoughts.

☐ b. Don't rock the boat.

☐ c. Everyone knows that the natural world is perfect as it is.

5. What did you have to do to answer question 3?

☒ a. find a cause (why something happened)

☐ b. find an opinion (what someone thinks about something)

☐ c. find a contrast (how things are different)

___5___ Number of correct answers

Record your personal assessment of your work on the Critical Thinking Chart on page 58.

Personal Response

How do you think you would feel if the moon were destroyed?

___[Think about how the destruction of the moon would change your life___

___and what your reaction to those changes might be. Write your answer___

___on the lines.]___

_____

_____

Self-Assessment

I was confused on question _____ in the _____ section

because _____

___[Choose one question that you found particularly hard to answer. Tell___

___why it confused or puzzled you.]___

_____

_____

Self-Assessment

To get the most out of the *Wild Side* series, you need to take charge of your own progress in improving your reading comprehension and critical thinking skills. Here are some of the features that help you work on those essential skills.

Reading Comprehension Exercises. Complete these exercises immediately after reading the article. They help you recall what you have read, understand the stated and implied main ideas, and add words to your working vocabulary.

Critical Thinking Skills Exercises. These exercises help you focus on the authors' approach and purpose, recognize and generate summaries and paraphrases, and identify relationships between ideas.

Personal Response and Self-Assessment. Questions in this category help you relate the articles to your personal experience and give you the opportunity to evaluate your understanding of the information in that lesson.

Compare and Contrast Charts. At the end of each unit you will complete a Compare and Contrast Chart. The completed chart helps you see what the articles have in common and gives you an opportunity to explore your own ideas about the topics discussed in the articles.

The Graphs. The graphs and charts at the end of each unit enable you to keep track of your progress. Check your graphs regularly with your teacher. Decide whether your progress is satisfactory or whether you need additional work on some skills. What types of exercises are you having difficulty with? Talk with your teacher about ways to work on the skills in which you need the most practice.

UNIT ONE

The Mysterious Life of Twins

Jim Lewis was an identical twin. But he hadn't seen his brother since birth. The two boys were adopted by different families. They knew nothing about each other. Yet when they were brought together in 1979 after 39 years, something spooky seemed to be going on. For one thing, both boys had been named James. Both went by the nickname "Jim."

Scientists have been exploring the relationship between twins for many years. They have studied pairs of twins who grew up together and other pairs who were separated at birth. They have come up with some remarkable findings.

As children, they both had a pet dog named Toy.

2   But that was only the beginning. Each Jim had married a woman named Linda. Each then had a son. One named his son James Alan. The other named his son James Allen. Later, both Jims got divorced. Each had remarried—and in both cases, the second wife's name was Betty! Each Jim drove the same kind of blue car. Each had the same favorite drink. Each bit his nails, liked woodworking, and took vacations to the very same beach in Florida!

3   Could all of this be coincidence? Or do twins share a special connection? Scientists have long known that identical twins have the same genes. But no one believed there was a gene that tells you what kind of car to buy. So what made the "Jim" twins live such similar lives?

4   In the past, people thought twins were alike simply because they grew up together. They saw the same people. They learned to like the same things. But that is not the case with the "Jim" twins. They did not grow up together. They knew nothing about each other when they bought cars, named their sons, and picked out beaches.

5   In the 1980s a man named Thomas J. Bouchard, Jr., took a closer look at twins. He found other sets of identical twins who had lived apart since birth. Among them were Daphne Goodship and Barbara Hebert. Like the "Jim" twins, these women had not seen each other for 39 years. Bouchard arranged for them to meet in London, England. At that meeting, Daphne and Barbara showed up wearing the same kind of clothes! Both had chosen a light brown dress and brown velvet jacket.

6   As the two women compared notes, they found they were alike in many ways. Both had the weird habit of pushing up their noses. Both had met their husbands at local dances when they were 16. Each of them had given birth to two sons, then a daughter. Strangest of all, each had fallen down the stairs at the age of 15. These accidents had left both twins with weak ankles.

7   Then there was Jack Yufe and Oskar Stöhr. Bouchard brought them together when they were 47 years old. It turned out that both men had short, clipped mustaches. Both wore rectangular wire-rimmed glasses. And both showed up at their first meeting wearing the same kind of fancy blue shirt. Jack and Oskar soon found more "coincidences." They walked with the same kind of swinging steps. They shared the habit of keeping extra rubber bands around their wrists. Both of them read magazines from back to front. They both even had the odd habit of flushing a toilet before using it!

8   The twins in Bouchard's study were more alike than anyone would have guessed. None of them had been in touch with his or her twin growing up. So what led them to make so many of the same choices in life? Some people think twins can communicate with each other in mysterious ways. Ron and Rod Fuller are identical twins from Dallas, Texas. They say each can tell when the other one is in trouble. Explains Rod, "There is a certain bond that we have for one another that I think all twins have."

9   Other twins agree. Andreina and Andreini McPherson grew up in

Chino Hills, California. They say they, too, can each tell how the other is feeling. In fact, they claim, they can feel each other's pain. When one of them is hurt, the other one can feel the injury.

10   If that is true, then maybe twins raised apart can also communicate in special ways. Did the twins from Bouchard's study send each other messages for years without knowing it? Perhaps. But it may be that the answer lies in the genes, after all. In 1988 Dr. David Teplica began to study twins. He took pictures of six thousand pairs of identical twins. He found some amazing things. These twins had freckles in the same spots. They got gray hairs at the same time and in the same places on their heads. Their faces got the same wrinkles. They even got pimples on their noses on exactly the same day! To Dr. Teplica, there was just one way to explain all this. Genes had to be controlling these events.

11   It's hard to believe we are born with genes that control when and where we get pimples. But that may be the case. Thomas Bouchard says his work also points to the power of genes. He believes genes explain many of the "coincidences" among the twins he studied. So who knows? Maybe there really is a gene that tells us what kind of car to buy.

If you have been timed while reading this article, enter your reading time below. Then turn to the Words-per-Minute Table on page 55 and look up your reading speed (words per minute). Enter your reading speed on the graph on page 56.

Reading Time: Lesson 1

_____ : _____

Minutes   Seconds

A | Finding the Main Idea

One statement below expresses the main idea of the article. One statement is too general, or too broad. The other statement explains only part of the article; it is too narrow. Label the statements using the following key:

M—Main Idea   **B—Too Broad**   **N—Too Narrow**

_____ 1. There seems to be a special connection between twins, perhaps one that is related to their shared genes.

_____ 2. Jim Lewis and his twin brother lived surprisingly similar lives, from the names of their children to their choice of cars.

_____ 3. The study of twins has led to some interesting discoveries.

_____ Score 15 points for a correct M answer.

_____ Score 5 points for each correct B or N answer.

_____ **Total Score:** Finding the Main Idea

B | Recalling Facts

How well do you remember the facts in the article? Put an X in the box next to the answer that correctly completes each statement about the article.

1. Scientists have long known that identical twins
   - ☐ a. share the same genes.
   - ☐ b. live identical lives.
   - ☐ c. are always lifelong friends.

2. When twins Daphne Goodship and Barbara Hebert met for the first time in London, they both
   - ☐ a. were late for the meeting.
   - ☐ b. wore the same kind of clothes.
   - ☐ c. had the same haircut.

3. Rod Fuller, a twin from Texas, says all twins have
   - ☐ a. similar likes and dislikes.
   - ☐ b. curiosity about the world.
   - ☐ c. a certain bond for one another.

4. Dr. Teplica says twins' similarities are caused by
   - ☐ a. the genes they share.
   - ☐ b. shared experiences as they grow up.
   - ☐ c. coincidence.

5. Andreina and Andreini McPherson claim that when one of them gets hurt, the other
   - ☐ a. gets hurt the same way on the next day.
   - ☐ b. calls her on the phone.
   - ☐ c. can feel her pain.

Score 5 points for each correct answer.

_____ **Total Score:** Recalling Facts

C Making Inferences

When you combine your own experience and information from a text to draw a conclusion that is not directly stated in that text, you are making an inference. Below are five statements that may or may not be inferences based on information in the article. Label the statements using the following key:

C—Correct Inference   F—Faulty Inference

_____ 1. Pairs of identical twins have the same taste in clothes.

_____ 2. There is a good chance that an identical twin will look more like her twin than like her other sisters.

_____ 3. Separating identical twins at birth has no effect on their closeness and friendship later in life.

_____ 4. If you keep in touch with your twin, the two of you will probably begin to look alike and act alike.

_____ 5. Many of the changes that take place in our bodies are caused by genes.

Score 5 points for each correct answer.

_____ **Total Score:** Making Inferences

D Using Words Precisely

Each numbered sentence below contains an underlined word or phrase from the article. Following the sentence are three definitions. One definition is closest to the meaning of the underlined word. One definition is opposite or nearly opposite. Label those two definitions using the following key; do not label the remaining definition.

C—Closest   O—Opposite or Nearly Opposite

1. Could all of this be a coincidence?

_____ a. chance event

_____ b. planned event

_____ c. joke

2. Both had the weird habit of pushing up their noses.

_____ a. common

_____ b. unpleasant

_____ c. odd

3. Some people think twins can communicate with each other in mysterious ways.

_____ a. keep things secret

_____ b. make things known

_____ c. quarrel

4. There is a certain bond that we have for one another that I think all twins have.

_____ a. name

_____ b. division

_____ c. link

5. He found some <u>amazing</u> things.

_____ a. dull and normal

_____ b. incredible

_____ c. similar

_____ Score 3 points for each correct C answer.

_____ Score 2 points for each correct O answer.

_____ **Total Score:** Using Words Precisely

Enter the four total scores in the spaces below, and add them together to find your Reading Comprehension Score. Then record your score on the graph on page 57.

Score	Question Type	Lesson 1
_____	Finding the Main Idea	
_____	Recalling Facts	
_____	Making Inferences	
_____	Using Words Precisely	
_____	**Reading Comprehension Score**	

Author's Approach

Put an X in the box next to the correct answer.

1. What is the authors' purpose in writing "The Mysterious Life of Twins"?

☐ a. to convey a mood of suspense

☐ b. to inform the reader about amazing similarities between twins and to suggest a reason for them

☐ c. to describe a situation in which people met family members after many years apart

2. From the statements below, choose those that you believe the authors would agree with.

☐ a. Twins often seem to be strongly connected to each other even if they have never lived together.

☐ b. Genes may have something to do with the strange similarities between twins.

☐ c. All similarities between twins can be explained by coincidence.

3. Choose the statement below that best describes the authors' position in paragraph 11.

☐ a. Maybe genes control more about our lives than we thought possible.

☐ b. No sensible person thinks that coincidences among twins can be explained by genes.

☐ c. Every human is born with similar genes.

_____ Number of correct answers

Record your personal assessment of your work on the Critical Thinking Chart on page 58.

Summarizing and Paraphrasing

Follow the directions provided for question 1. Put an X in the box next to the correct answer for the other questions.

1. Look for the important ideas and events in paragraphs 8 and 9. Summarize those paragraphs in one or two sentences.

_____

_____

_____

_____

2. Below are summaries of the article. Choose the summary that says all the most important things about the article in the fewest words.

☐ a. The study of twins may reveal some interesting facts about all of us, from what clothes we wear to what kind of car we drive.

☐ b. Although people used to think that twins were alike only because they grew up together, recent research suggests other reasons for the similarities.

☐ c. Twins who have always lived apart sometimes are eerily similar. These similarities suggest that genes are responsible for what happens to our bodies and for many of our decisions.

3. Choose the sentence that correctly restates the following sentence from the article: "The twins in Bouchard's study were more alike than anyone would have guessed."

☐ a. No one would have predicted that the twins Bouchard studied would be so similar.

☐ b. The twins in Bouchard's study guessed that they would be alike.

☐ c. Bouchard himself guessed that the twins in his study would be amazingly similar.

_____ Number of correct answers

Record your personal assessment of your work on the Critical Thinking Chart on page 58.

Critical Thinking

Put an X in the box next to the correct answer for questions 1, 2, and 4. Follow the directions provided for the other questions.

1. Which of the following statements from the article is an opinion rather than a fact?

☐ a. In 1988 Dr. David Teplica began to study twins. He took pictures of six thousand pairs of identical twins.

☐ b. At that meeting, Daphne and Barbara showed up wearing the same kind of clothes!

☐ c. If that is true, then maybe twins raised apart can also communicate in special ways.

2. From what the article told about what researchers have learned about twins, you can predict that scientists will

☐ a. stop doing research on twins.

☐ b. continue to do research about twins.

☐ c. show that all the research done on twins has been fake.

3. Choose from the letters below to correctly complete the following statement. Write the letters on the lines.

   In the article, Daphne Goodship and Barbara Hebert's _____ and _____ are alike.

   a. husbands' names

   b. accidents at the age of 15

   c. habit of pushing up their noses

4. If you were a scientist, how could you use the information in the article to learn more about how genes affect human lives?

☐ a. Like scientists in the article, I would study twins.

☐ b. I would separate all sets of twins at birth.

☐ c. I would decide that everything about us is determined by our genes.

5. Which paragraphs from the article provide evidence that supports your answer to question 3? _____

_____ Number of correct answers

Record your personal assessment of your work on the Critical Thinking Chart on page 58.

Personal Response

If you could ask the authors of the article one question, what would it be?

_____

_____

_____

Self-Assessment

From reading this article, I have learned _____

_____

_____

_____

Is the Earth Alive?

Imagine drilling a hole eight miles deep. That's what Arthur Conan Doyle described in his short story titled "When the World Screamed." In Doyle's story, drilling that hole turned out to be a bad idea. As the hole got deeper and deeper, the earth began to howl in pain.

2 Doyle's story was pure science fiction, of course. But some scientists think his image comes pretty close to the truth. These people say that our

How can we tell that something is alive? It reacts to its surroundings, and if it senses danger it runs away or defends itself. It responds to food and light. It does what it can to keep itself alive. Can Earth itself be classified as a living being? Some scientists think so.

planet really is alive. It may not actually scream in pain. But it can and it does react to what we humans do.

3   The concept of the earth being alive may sound crazy. Most of us think of our planet as a kind of giant rock spinning through space. It is true that living creatures swarm all over this rock. But the rock itself is not alive. Or is it?

4   Dr. James Lovelock says it is. Lovelock is a British scientist. He calls his belief *Gaia* [pronounced guy-ah]. That means "Mother Earth" in Greek. Lovelock has written two books to explain his position. In 1979 he wrote *Gaia*. Nine years later he wrote *The Ages of Gaia*. "You may find it hard to swallow," Lovelock said, ". . . that anything as large and apparently [dead] as the Earth is alive." Yet that's how Lovelock sees it. And he's not the first one to look at things this way. A German scientist named Gustav Fechner (1801–1887) thought everything was alive.

5   Fechner believed that all planets have a life of their own. In fact, he claimed, a planet is a higher form of life than you and I. As proof, Fechner noted that the earth doesn't have arms and legs. Why? According to Fechner, the earth doesn't need them. The planet Earth already has everything it desires. Human beings, on the other hand, are not born with everything they need. They must find ways to feed and shelter themselves. So they have had to develop arms and legs in order to do that.

6   Fechner's weird view didn't catch on during his lifetime. Other scientists simply ignored him. They went on thinking of the earth as a mixture of lava, rocks, water, soil, and plants. To be sure, these scientists said, the earth is a wonderful place. But it is not "alive" in any true sense of the word.

7   Then along came Lovelock. His bold views caught many people's attention. Even some scientists became interested in Gaia. Lovelock says Gaia is based on one key principle. It is this: Living things and the earth have a direct effect on each other. At first, that might not sound like a shocking idea. After all, it is clear that the earth affects life. There is no argument here. People who live in the cold mountains do things one way. Those who live in the warm tropics do things another way. Those who live in a desert do things a third way. So the conditions offered by the earth do indeed affect how we live.

8   But Lovelock believes the reverse is true as well. He says that life affects the earth. To show this, he built a simple model of the world. He called it Daisyworld. The main form of life in this model world is black and white daisies. The daisies grow when it is warm and die when it is cold. But if it gets too hot or too cold, the daisies can fight back. They can get the earth to change its temperature. If the sunlight is weak, more black daisies will grow. Their black petals absorb the sunlight. This tends to warm the earth. If the sunlight is strong, more white daisies will grow. Their white petals then reflect the sunlight, which will cool the earth.

9   In the real world, says Lovelock, the same thing happens. Humans and other forms of life constantly cause the earth to react to what they do. Followers of Gaia believe that some of these reactions have been pretty strong. They say the earth has changed its temperature. They say it

has changed the level of salt in the oceans. They even say it has moved continents around.

10   That does not mean humans have all the power. Lovelock notes that Mother Earth is one tough old lady. She can take a lot of abuse. After all, during her long history the earth has lived through ice ages, earthquakes, and volcanoes. The earth has even survived direct hits from meteors. It is not likely to experience anything worse. In light of what this planet has already endured, Lovelock says, a nuclear war would be "as trivial as a summer breeze."

11   Does this mean it doesn't matter if we blow ourselves up? That's right.

Gaia followers say that if this happened, the earth itself would go right on living. And sooner or later, some other form of life would take our place. Lovelock even thinks he knows what that life form would be—whales! He says whales have brain power far beyond what we have imagined.

12   Many people still think Lovelock and his followers are loony. Still, Gaia has a magical ring to it. The idea is catching on. There have been dozens of articles written about it. There have been Gaia lectures. There have been Gaia films. A 1984 book on Gaia sold more than 175,000 copies. No one yet claims to have heard the earth

crying out like it did in Doyle's story. But maybe, just maybe, we're not listening hard enough.

If you have been timed while reading this article, enter your reading time below. Then turn to the Words-per-Minute Table on page 55 and look up your reading speed (words per minute). Enter your reading speed on the graph on page 56.

Reading Time: Lesson 2

_____ : _____
Minutes   *Seconds*

A Finding the Main Idea

One statement below expresses the main idea of the article. One statement is too general, or too broad. The other statement explains only part of the article; it is too narrow. Label the statements using the following key:

M—Main Idea   **B—Too Broad**   **N—Too Narrow**

_____ 1. Not all scientists agree with Dr. James Lovelock on the nature of the planet Earth.

_____ 2. Dr. James Lovelock calls his concept *Gaia,* meaning "Mother Earth" in Greek.

_____ 3. The Gaia concept says that Earth reacts like a living being to changing conditions.

_____ Score 15 points for a correct M answer.

_____ Score 5 points for each correct B or N answer.

_____ **Total Score:** Finding the Main Idea

B Recalling Facts

How well do you remember the facts in the article? Put an X in the box next to the answer that correctly completes each statement about the article.

1. Dr. James Lovelock is
   ☐ a. a writer of science fiction.
   ☐ b. an American scientist.
   ☐ c. a British scientist.

2. The German scientist Gustav Fechner believed that
   ☐ a. digging a deep hole can make Earth scream.
   ☐ b. planets are a higher life form than humans.
   ☐ c. anything as large as Earth is dead.

3. The principle underlying Gaia is that living things
   ☐ a. depend on Earth for their survival.
   ☐ b. must find ways to feed and shelter themselves.
   ☐ c. and Earth have a direct effect on each other.

4. If more black daisies grow on Earth, their petals absorb sunlight and
   ☐ a. Earth gets warmer.
   ☐ b. Earth gets cooler.
   ☐ c. there is no effect on Earth's temperature.

5. Followers of Gaia say that activity on Earth has
   ☐ a. brought on direct hits from meteors.
   ☐ b. caused changes in the level of salt in oceans.
   ☐ c. given humans power over the planet.

Score 5 points for each correct answer.

_____ **Total Score:** Recalling Facts

C Making Inferences

When you combine your own experience and information from a text to draw a conclusion that is not directly stated in that text, you are making an inference. Below are five statements that may or may not be inferences based on information in the article. Label the statements using the following key:

C—Correct Inference   **F—Faulty Inference**

_____ 1. Most science fiction writers believe in the Gaia concept.

_____ 2. What living things on Earth did during the last ice age may have caused Earth's temperature to rise, bringing an end to the Ice Age.

_____ 3. A person who believes in God could not believe in Gaia.

_____ 4. Even if Earth reacts to living creatures on its surface, it won't favor one life form over another.

_____ 5. People who believe in Gaia want to change human behavior in order to save the planet from death.

Score 5 points for each correct answer.

_____ **Total Score:** Making Inferences

D Using Words Precisely

Each numbered sentence below contains an underlined word or phrase from the article. Following the sentence are three definitions. One definition is closest to the meaning of the underlined word. One definition is opposite or nearly opposite. Label those two definitions using the following key; do not label the remaining definition.

C—Closest   **O—Opposite or Nearly Opposite**

1. But it can and does <u>react</u> to what we humans do.

_____ a. give no attention

_____ b. act in answer

_____ c. come closer

2. It is true that living creatures <u>swarm</u> all over this rock.

_____ a. crowd

_____ b. jog

_____ c. wait alone and unmoving

3. You may find it hard to <u>swallow</u> . . . that anything as large and apparently dead as the Earth is alive.

_____ a. reject

_____ b. describe

_____ c. accept

4. But Lovelock believes the <u>reverse</u> is true, as well.

_____ a. opposite

_____ b. same

_____ c. course

5. In light of what this planet has already endured, Lovelock says, a nuclear war would be "as <u>trivial</u> as a summer breeze."

_____ a. unlikely

_____ b. unimportant

_____ c. serious

_____ Score 3 points for each correct C answer.

_____ Score 2 points for each correct O answer.

_____ **Total Score:** Using Words Precisely

Enter the four total scores in the spaces below, and add them together to find your Reading Comprehension Score. Then record your score on the graph on page 57.

Score	Question Type	Lesson 2
_____	Finding the Main Idea	
_____	Recalling Facts	
_____	Making Inferences	
_____	Using Words Precisely	
_____	**Reading Comprehension Score**	

Author's Approach

Put an X in the box next to the correct answer.

1. The main purpose of the first paragraph is to

☐ a. introduce the idea that the earth may be alive.

☐ b. encourage the reader to read "When the World Screamed."

☐ c. make fun of the writing of Arthur Conan Doyle.

2. Which of the following statements from the article best describes the central idea of Gaia?

☐ a. The planet Earth already has everything it desires.

☐ b. Most of us think of our planet as a kind of giant rock spinning through space.

☐ c. Living things and the earth have a direct effect on each other.

3. Judging by statements from the article "Is the Earth Alive?" you can conclude that the authors want the reader to think that

☐ a. anyone who believes the Gaia theory is not thinking straight.

☐ b. the theory that the earth is alive may make some sense.

☐ c. the Gaia theory is accepted by most serious scientists.

4. Choose the statement below that is the weakest argument for believing that the earth is alive.

☐ a. The earth needs no arms or legs for feeding or sheltering itself.

☐ b. The earth constantly reacts to outside forces.

☐ c. The earth has the power to change its temperature and the amount of salt in its oceans.

_____ Number of correct answers

Record your personal assessment of your work on the Critical Thinking Chart on page 58.

Summarizing and Paraphrasing

Put an X in the box next to the correct answer for questions 1 and 3. Follow the directions provided for question 2.

1. Complete the following one-sentence summary of the article using the lettered phrases from the phrase bank below. Write the letters on the lines.

> **Phrase Bank:**
> a. Gustav Fechner's views about the earth
> b. current interest in Gaia
> c. Dr. James Lovelock's Gaia theory

   The article "Is the Earth Alive?" begins with _____, goes on to explain _____, and ends with _____.

2. Reread paragraph 10 in the article. Below, write a summary of the paragraph in no more than 25 words.

   _____

   _____

   _____

   _____

   Reread your summary and decide whether it covers the important ideas in the paragraph. Next, decide how to shorten the summary to 15 words or less without leaving out any essential information. Write this summary below.

   _____

   _____

   _____

3. Read the statement from the article below. Then read the paraphrase of that statement. Choose the reason that best tells why the paraphrase does not say the same thing as the statement.

   Statement: Lovelock believes that if people were to disappear from the earth, another life form would take their place.

   Paraphrase: According to Lovelock, whales would replace humans if people disappeared from the face of the earth.

   ☐ a. Paraphrase says too much.

   ☐ b. Paraphrase doesn't say enough.

   ☐ c. Paraphrase doesn't agree with the statement.

> _____ Number of correct answers
>
> Record your personal assessment of your work on the Critical Thinking Chart on page 58.

Critical Thinking

Follow the directions provided for questions 1, 3, 4, and 5. Put an X in the box next to the correct answer for question 2.

1. For each statement below, write *O* if it expresses an opinion or write *F* if it expresses a fact.

   _____ a. The earth has survived ice ages, earthquakes, and direct hits from meteors.

   _____ b. People who believe in Gaia will believe almost anything.

   _____ c. Dr. James Lovelock doesn't care whether anyone else believes his theory.

2. If Dr. Lovelock's theory is correct, you can predict that if humans were wiped out in a nuclear war,

☐ a. the earth would survive and maybe be taken over by a new life form.

☐ b. their absence would have no effect on the earth.

☐ c. the earth would not survive.

3. Choose from the letters below to correctly complete the following statement. Write the letters on the lines.

In the article, _____ and _____ are different.

a. Fechner's theories on whether or not the earth is alive

b. most people's view on whether or not the earth is alive

c. Lovelock's theories on whether or not the earth is alive

4. Choose from the letters below to correctly complete the following statement. Write the letters on the lines.

According to Lovelock's Daisyworld model, _____ would cause _____ to grow, and the effect would be that _____.

a. their petals would absorb sunlight and warm the earth

b. more black daisies

c. cold temperatures and weak sunlight

5. In which paragraph did you find your information or details to answer question 4? _____

_____ Number of correct answers

Record your personal assessment of your work on the Critical Thinking Chart on page 58.

Personal Response

I disagree with the authors because _____

_____

_____

_____

Self-Assessment

The part I found most difficult about the article was _____

_____

_____

I found this difficult because _____

_____

_____

_____

_____

Great Balls of Fire

"I saw a great big shining light," said Betty Barrett. "It hurt your eyes to look at it." Frightened, she rushed to a friend's house. "I felt foolish," she later said. "If I hadn't [seen] it, I guess I wouldn't have believed it either. But it was the brightest thing that I'd ever seen."

2   Barrett and her friend went out to look again for the shining light. This time they saw nothing. But just as the women turned to go inside the house, something blew up. They saw an

We are all familiar with the sight of lightning zigzagging across a stormy sky. Some people have had close encounters with another form of lightning, but what it is and where it comes from is still a mystery.

enormous flash of fire. Then, just as quickly as it had appeared, it was gone. Later, the fire department checked for signs of a fire. It found nothing. Not a single blade of grass had been burned.

3   This happened in 1976 in Virginia. Seven years later a ball of fire entered a Russian jet. It was just four inches across. According to one report, it "flew above the heads of the stunned passengers." When it reached the tail, it split in two. Then the two parts "joined together again and left the plane." Mechanics later found two holes in the jet—one in the front and one in the tail.

4   In 1999 a Pennsylvania woman was sitting in her living room. Looking out the window, she saw the rain coming down. She heard thunder and saw lightning. Then out of the corner of her eye, she saw what looked like a green ball. "It was floating about 25 to 30 feet above the street. It was about the size of a basketball. . . . All of a sudden, it grew brighter and larger and then burst in the air." Two minutes later the power in her house went out.

5   What was going on? What were these balls of fire that seemed to come

out of nowhere? And why did they disappear so quickly? No one knows for sure. But stories like these have been around for centuries.

6   Usually the balls come and go within a few seconds and leave without doing any harm. But they have been known to float up chimneys and explode halfway up. And, as in the case of the Russian jet, they have burned holes through things.

7   These weird balls of fire are known as ball lightning. For a long time scientists scoffed at ball lightning. They said it didn't exist. Ball lightning didn't obey the known laws of science. So scientists thought it had to be just a figment of people's imagination.

8   Besides, there were many different reports of ball lightning. Some people said the balls of fire exploded. Others claimed the balls vanished without a sound. Still others heard a hissing noise. Most people said the ball lightning floated with the wind. But some people saw it go into the wind. Some saw it slip through cracks or go up the chimney. A few even saw it go through walls. Then there was the question of color. Some people said it

was green. Others said it was blue or red or yellow.

9   All the eyewitnesses had been startled by what they had seen. Scientists figured that affected how people "saw" things. Also, there was the time factor. The balls came and went very quickly. Most lingered just a few seconds. They never stayed long enough for anyone to study. Given this, it is no wonder that scientists responded to ball lightning stories with a sigh and, "Oh, sure. Right."

10   Scientists know that the eye can play tricks. People can "see" things that are not really there. Think about what happens when you look at a flashbulb as it goes off. The flash is over in an instant. But your eye still sees a glow from the flash. In short, you still see the light after the source of the light is gone.

11   Is that what happens with ball lightning? Some scientists think so. Ball lightning is usually seen in a thunderstorm. Normal lightning can act just like a flashbulb. It creates an afterimage in the brain. If you focus your mind on it, the afterimage tends to float around. It looks a lot like ball lightning. Also, afterimages last about as long as ball lightning. They have the same colors and shapes. And they leave having done no damage.

12   So is ball lightning just an afterimage in the brain? Many of the facts suggest that it is. But there are other facts that just don't fit so neatly. An afterimage doesn't explode. It doesn't make a hissing sound. It doesn't burn holes. And it doesn't knock out the power in a house. Also, how could the passengers on the Russian jet all have the same afterimage?

13   Scientists don't like to admit when they're wrong. But, in this case, they have done so. Many now accept ball lightning as real. They believe most of the reports are true. But they still don't know exactly what ball lightning is. There are many theories, but none that all people accept. Some scientists think it is caused by strange gases. Others think it is linked to earthquakes. Still others think it might be caused by small nuclear reactions.

14   In 2000 a new theory popped up. Two scientists suggested that ball lightning might be caused by burning silicon. Silicon can be found in soil mixture. When a lightning bolt hits the ground, it produces great heat. If the soil mixture contains the right amount of silicon, the bolt will release tiny bits of silicon in the air. The bits might then form chains in the air. The chains,

in turn, could create puffy clusters that float. The clusters then oxidize, or burn up. If the heat of the ball is low, it will fade away. If it is high, it will explode.

15   The two scientists have not yet proved their theory. So in the world of science, it remains just a theory. But the existence of ball lightning seems pretty certain. So if you ever see this kind of weird fireball, you can relax. It's not your eyes playing tricks on you. And you're not crazy.

If you have been timed while reading this article, enter your reading time below. Then turn to the Words-per-Minute Table on page 55 and look up your reading speed (words per minute). Enter your reading speed on the graph on page 56.

Reading Time: Lesson 3

_____ : _____
Minutes   *Seconds*

A | Finding the Main Idea

One statement below expresses the main idea of the article. One statement is too general, or too broad. The other statement explains only part of the article; it is too narrow. Label the statements using the following key:

M—Main Idea   **B—Too Broad**   **N—Too Narrow**

_____ 1. Ball lightning is a strange phenomenon that scientists still haven't figured out.

_____ 2. Ball lightning appears as a ball that floats in the air and disappears quickly. Scientists who used to scoff at the idea are now admitting it exists.

_____ 3. According to two scientists, ball lightning happens when regular lightning hits the ground and releases silicon bits that then burn up.

_____ Score 15 points for a correct M answer.

_____ Score 5 points for each correct B or N answer.

_____ **Total Score:** Finding the Main Idea

B | Recalling Facts

How well do you remember the facts in the article? Put an X in the box next to the answer that correctly completes each statement about the article.

1. Where Betty Barrett saw a shining light explode, the fire department found
   - ☐ a. an area of burned grass.
   - ☐ b. two holes in the ground.
   - ☐ c. nothing extraordinary.

2. In 1983 a ball of lightning aboard a Russian jet created
   - ☐ a. a hissing noise.
   - ☐ b. two holes in the jet.
   - ☐ c. a huge explosion.

3. The ball lightning that appeared on the Russian jet was about
   - ☐ a. four inches across.
   - ☐ b. one foot across.
   - ☐ c. four feet across.

4. In 2000 two scientists suggested that ball lightning is made of burning
   - ☐ a. oxygen.
   - ☐ b. silicon.
   - ☐ c. nitrogen.

5. According to the article, some scientists think ball lightning is somehow connected with
   - ☐ a. floods.
   - ☐ b. volcanoes.
   - ☐ c. earthquakes.

Score 5 points for each correct answer.

_____ **Total Score:** Recalling Facts

C   Making Inferences

When you combine your own experience with information from a text to draw a conclusion that is not directly stated in that text, you are making an inference. Below are five statements that may or may not be inferences based on information in the article. Label the statements using the following key:

C—Correct Inference   **F—Faulty Inference**

_____ 1. Many people on the Russian jet became nervous or afraid when the ball of lightning passed through the cabin.

_____ 2. All of the important laws of nature are known and understood by scientists.

_____ 3. Any theory that has not been proven is false.

_____ 4. Scientists have great respect for the observations and theories of nonscientists.

_____ 5. Scientists are slow to believe in something they can't observe and study carefully over time.

Score 5 points for each correct answer.

_____ **Total Score:** Making Inferences

D   Using Words Precisely

Each numbered sentence below contains an underlined word or phrase from the article. Following the sentence are three definitions. One definition is closest to the meaning of the underlined word. One definition is opposite or nearly opposite. Label those two definitions using the following key; do not label the remaining definition.

C—Closest   **O—Opposite or Nearly Opposite**

1. They saw an <u>enormous</u> flash of fire.

_____ a. dangerous

_____ b. huge

_____ c. tiny

2. According to one report, it "flew above the heads of the <u>stunned</u> passengers."

_____ a. shocked

_____ b. unsuspecting

_____ c. bored

3. The flash is over in an <u>instant</u>.

_____ a. long period of time

_____ b. different place

_____ c. short period of time

4. Normal lightning can act just like a flashbulb. It creates an <u>afterimage</u> in the brain.

_____ a. malfunction or error

_____ b. visual sensation that continues after the image is no longer visible

_____ c. visual sensation that comes before actually seeing an image

5. The chains, in turn, could create puffy <u>clusters</u> that float.

_____ a. individuals acting alone

_____ b. collections or groups

_____ c. waves

_____ Score 3 points for each correct C answer.

_____ Score 2 points for each correct O answer.

_____ **Total Score:** Using Words Precisely

Enter the four total scores in the spaces below, and add them together to find your Reading Comprehension Score. Then record your score on the graph on page 57.

Score	Question Type	Lesson 3
_____	Finding the Main Idea	
_____	Recalling Facts	
_____	Making Inferences	
_____	Using Words Precisely	
_____	**Reading Comprehension Score**	

Author's Approach

Put an X in the box next to the correct answer.

1. The authors use the first sentence of the article to

☐ a. describe ball lightning.

☐ b. compare ball lightning and regular lightning.

☐ c. entertain the reader with an interesting story.

2. What do the authors mean by the statement "But stories like these [sightings of balls of fire] have been around for centuries"?

☐ a. Storytellers of the past made up these tales about balls of fire, and people have been repeating them for centuries.

☐ b. No one took the stories about balls of fire seriously centuries ago, and certainly no one takes them seriously today.

☐ c. It seems that ball lightning is not a new phenomenon.

3. Some scientists think that ball lightning is simply an afterimage in the brain. Choose the statement below that best explains how the authors address the opposing point of view in the article.

☐ a. The authors note that afterimages last about as long as ball lightning is reported to last.

☐ b. The authors point out that afterimages seem to float around the same as ball lightning does.

☐ c. The authors point out that an afterimage doesn't make noise, explode, or burn holes as ball lightning does.

_____ Number of correct answers

Record your personal assessment of your work on the Critical Thinking Chart on page 58.

Summarizing and Paraphrasing

Follow the directions provided for questions 1 and 2. Put an X in the box next to the correct answer for question 3.

1. Look for the important ideas and events in paragraphs 1 and 2. Summarize those paragraphs in one or two sentences.

_____

_____

_____

2. Complete the following one-sentence summary of the article using the lettered phrases from the phrase bank below. Write the letters on the lines.

> **Phrase Bank:**
> a. descriptions of ball lightning
> b. detailed reports of specific sightings of ball lightning
> c. scientific theories about ball lightning

The article about ball lightning begins with _____, goes on to explain _____, and ends with _____.

3. Read the statement from the article below. Then read the paraphrase of that statement. Choose the reason that best tells why the paraphrase does not say the same thing as the statement.

   Statement: Often the eye continues to see a glow even after a flash of light is gone.

   Paraphrase: An afterimage is a glow that the eye continues to see despite the fact that the light is no longer shining.

☐ a. Paraphrase says too much.

☐ b. Paraphrase doesn't say enough.

☐ c. Paraphrase doesn't agree with the statement.

> _____ Number of correct answers
>
> Record your personal assessment of your work on the Critical Thinking Chart on page 58.

Critical Thinking

Put an X in the box next to the correct answer for questions 1 and 2. Follow the directions provided for the other questions.

1. Which of the following statements from the article is an opinion rather than a fact?

☐ a. Scientists don't like to admit when they're wrong.

☐ b. Usually the balls come and go within a few seconds and leave without doing any harm.

☐ c. Silicon can be found in soil mixture.

2. From what the article told about the two scientists who had the theory about ball lightning, you can predict that

☐ a. they will lose interest in proving their theory and abandon it very soon.

☐ b. they will continue trying to prove their theory.

☐ c. other scientists will stop them from doing research to prove their theory because they believe the theory is worthless.

CRITICAL THINKING

3. Choose from the letters below to correctly complete the following statement. Write the letters on the lines.

In the article, the way _____ and the way _____ are alike.

   a. ball lightning moves

   b. an afterimage moves

   c. regular lightning moves

4. Reread paragraph 14. Then choose from the letters below to correctly complete the following statement. Write the letters on the lines.

According to paragraph 14, _____ because _____.

   a. a lightning bolt has hit the earth and heated the soil mixture

   b. two scientists suggested a new theory

   c. silicon clusters may float in the air and then oxidize

5. In which paragraph did you find your information or details to answer question 3? _____

_____ Number of correct answers

Record your personal assessment of your work on the Critical Thinking Chart on page 58.

Personal Response

I know the feeling that Betty Barrett had when she called her neighbor to see the light, and for a while they saw nothing,

because _____

_____

_____

_____

Self-Assessment

While reading the article, I found it easiest to _____

_____

_____

_____

Firestorms

Legend says that it all began with a cow. On October 8, 1871, Mrs. O'Leary's cow knocked over a lantern in a barn.

A fire broke out. Soon most of Chicago was going up in flames. The damage was immense. Fire destroyed more than two thousand acres of the city. More than one hundred thousand people lost their homes. About 300 people died in the inferno. The Great Chicago Fire of 1871 shocked the nation. It became the most famous fire in American history.

As deadly and destructive as this blaze is, it cannot compare to the fury of a fire storm. A true firestorm is so intense that fire fighters have no effect on it. It destroys everything and everyone nearby, and it burns until nothing is left to burn. Luckily, a firestorm occurs only under special conditions.

2   And yet, on the same day, there was a fire in Wisconsin that was even worse. People did not hear about this second fire right away. The Great Chicago Fire was the hot news story of the day. Besides, the second fire took place in the small lumber town of Peshtigo. It took several days for word from this town to reach the outside world.

3   Peshtigo had seen plenty of fires before. Dense woods surrounded the town. Brush fires often broke out. The people of Peshtigo knew how to deal with them. This fire, though, was impossible to control. About 9:30 P.M., someone saw a dull red glow in the distance. That was followed by a low rumbling sound. Everyone in town knew exactly what that meant. The men jumped into action. The women got the children out of bed and dressed them. By 10 o'clock, the woods had turned bright crimson as flames leaped from tree to tree. Sparks flew everywhere. Soon the blaze reached the town itself. The wooden sidewalks caught fire. Sawdust used in the streets to keep the dust down also burst into flames. The angry blaze engulfed one building after another.

4   There was no hope of stopping the fire. The people just tried to save themselves. Some sought shelter in large buildings. But as the buildings went up in flames, most of these people burned to death. Others drowned after leaping into the river. Three people jumped into a large water tank at a sawmill. But even they did not survive. The fire turned the water so hot that everyone in the tank died.

5   The Peshtigo fire destroyed every building in town. About 800 people died. That was 500 more people than the Great Chicago Fire killed. In terms of lost lives, then, the Peshtigo fire was much worse than the one in Chicago.

6   The fame of the Chicago fire is well earned. It was, after all, a truly massive blaze. But it was a regular fire. The one in Peshtigo, on the other hand, was a rare kind of fire. It was actually a "firestorm." People who survived it talked of winds that were "tornado-like." They said balls of fire seemed to jump out of nowhere. These balls appeared and disappeared like lightning.

7   What is the difference between a normal fire and a firestorm? A normal fire is largely controlled by the weather.

High winds can fan the flames. In fact, strong, gusty winds did help to spread the Chicago fire. Similarly, a heavy rain can douse a normal fire. For example, rain often checks forest fires. A firestorm, on the other hand, *creates* its own weather. It makes its *own* wind and rain. A firestorm can make rain fall and lightning flash even on a sunny day. It can create small tornadoes, or whirls, filled with fire and deadly gases. These little weather systems grow inside a plume of smoke that rises high above the ground.

8   Firestorms are rare. The conditions have to be just right to create one. First, the fire must be really hot. That means having lots of fuel such as dry wood, sawdust, twigs, or brush. Second, the winds in the area must be weak. A strong wind would blow the rising smoke across the land and keep a plume from developing. Third, the air must be fairly warm. Warm air forms currents that rise into the upper atmosphere. Cold air sinks. Cold air

would press down on the plume and keep it from growing.

9   If the conditions are met, watch out. A billowing plume develops. It carries heat, smoke, ash, and gases higher and higher. Within this plume, the wind whips around at very high speeds. This wind turns into small but deadly tornadoes. The tornadoes can be as high as 400 feet and as wide as 50 feet. They travel at speeds of just six or seven miles an hour. But it's hard to tell where they'll go next.

10   As the plume rises, moisture in the air starts to condense on the ash and smoke particles. This creates a cloud that looks like a towering black storm cloud. A 1993 firestorm in Santa Barbara, California, created such a cloud. It reached 38,000 feet. That's almost two miles higher than Mount Everest!

11   As the cloud grows, more and more moisture condenses on the ash and smoke particles. Soon rain starts to fall. In that way, a firestorm creates its own

rainfall. The Santa Barbara firestorm produced lightning and almost half an inch of rain. But such rain rarely puts out the fire. One reason is that the plume doesn't stay perfectly straight. The upper part, where the rain forms, drifts slowly away from the source of the fire. So the rain doesn't fall on the fire itself. As a result, most firestorms don't put themselves out. They die only when their fuel supply runs out.

If you have been timed while reading this article, enter your reading time below. Then turn to the Words-per-Minute Table on page 55 and look up your reading speed (words per minute). Enter your reading speed on the graph on page 56.

Reading Time: Lesson 4

_____ : _____
Minutes   Seconds

A | Finding the Main Idea

One statement below expresses the main idea of the article. One statement is too general, or too broad. The other statement explains only part of the article; it is too narrow. Label the statements using the following key:

M—Main Idea   **B—Too Broad**   **N—Too Narrow**

_____ 1. Firestorms such as the one in Peshtigo in 1871 are a special kind of fire.

_____ 2. A firestorm destroyed the small lumber town of Peshtigo in October 1871, on the same day as the Great Chicago Fire.

_____ 3. Firestorms are more dangerous than regular fires because they make their own weather and cannot be controlled.

_____ Score 15 points for a correct M answer.

_____ Score 5 points for each correct B or N answer.

_____ **Total Score:** Finding the Main Idea

B | Recalling Facts

How well do you remember the facts in the article? Put an X in the box next to the answer that correctly completes each statement about the article.

1. Fires often started near Peshtigo because the
   - ☐ a. town was near Chicago.
   - ☐ b. town was surrounded by dense woods.
   - ☐ c. people of the town were careless.

2. In a regular fire, heavy winds can
   - ☐ a. put out the fire.
   - ☐ b. start the fire.
   - ☐ c. spread the fire.

3. The plume of a firestorm can reach heights of about
   - ☐ a. 40,000 feet.
   - ☐ b. 2,000 feet.
   - ☐ c. 400 feet.

4. One of the conditions that must be met before a firestorm can develop is
   - ☐ a. fairly warm air.
   - ☐ b. strong winds.
   - ☐ c. a cold weather front.

5. As the plume rises, moisture in the air
   - ☐ a. turns to ice.
   - ☐ b. disappears in the heat from the fire.
   - ☐ c. condenses on the ash and smoke particles.

Score 5 points for each correct answer.

_____ **Total Score:** Recalling Facts

C | Making Inferences

When you combine your own experience and information from a text to draw a conclusion that is not directly stated in that text, you are making an inference. Below are five statements that may or may not be inferences based on information in the article. Label the statements using the following key:

C—Correct Inference   F—Faulty Inference

_____ 1. The citizens of Peshtigo knew the roles they were to play whenever fire broke out.

_____ 2. News did not travel as fast in 1871 as it does today.

_____ 3. It is likely that you will see several firestorms in your lifetime.

_____ 4. Most tornadoes are caused by firestorms.

_____ 5. In a desert area without brush or dry wood, a firestorm would probably not develop.

Score 5 points for each correct answer.

_____ **Total Score:** Making Inferences

D | Using Words Precisely

Each numbered sentence below contains an underlined word or phrase from the article. Following the sentence are three definitions. One definition is closest to the meaning of the underlined word. One definition is opposite or nearly opposite. Label those two definitions using the following key; do not label the remaining definition.

C—Closest   O—Opposite or Nearly Opposite

1. It was after all, a truly <u>massive</u> blaze.

_____ a. huge

_____ b. terrifying

_____ c. tiny

2. People who <u>survived</u> it talked of winds that were "tornado-like."

_____ a. died in

_____ b. remembered

_____ c. lived through

3. For example, rain often <u>checks</u> forest fires.

_____ a. stops

_____ b. encourages

_____ c. goes along with

4. This creates a cloud that looks like a <u>towering</u> black storm cloud.

_____ a. short

_____ b. tall

_____ c. fast-moving

5. The Great Chicago Fire of 1871 <u>shocked</u> the nation.

_____ a. disturbed

_____ b. fooled

_____ c. bored

_____ Score 3 points for each correct C answer.

_____ Score 2 points for each correct O answer.

_____ **Total Score:** Using Words Precisely

Enter the four total scores in the spaces below, and add them together to find your Reading Comprehension Score. Then record your score on the graph on page 57.

Score	Question Type	Lesson 4
_____	Finding the Main Idea	
_____	Recalling Facts	
_____	Making Inferences	
_____	Using Words Precisely	
_____	**Reading Comprehension Score**	

Author's Approach

Put an X in the box next to the correct answer.

1. The authors use the first sentence of the article to

☐ a. inform the reader of how dangerous cows can be.

☐ b. warn the reader that what follows may not be factual.

☐ c. begin the article with a true story.

2. Judging by statements from the article "Firestorms," you can conclude that the authors want the reader to think that

☐ a. the fire in Peshtigo was worse than the Chicago fire.

☐ b. the fire that destroyed Peshtigo was more unusual than the one that hit Chicago.

☐ c. the Peshtigo fire wasn't as interesting as the one that destroyed Chicago.

3. What do the authors imply by saying "It took several days for word from this town [Peshtigo] to reach the outside world"?

☐ a. No one in Peshtigo survived the firestorm.

☐ b. The people of Peshtigo didn't care whether anyone else knew about their tragedy.

☐ c. In general, communication and travel was slower 1871 than it is today.

4. The authors probably wrote this article to

☐ a. inform readers about an unusual natural event.

☐ b. show that Peshtigo's fire should have been given more attention than it was given in 1871.

☐ c. persuade towns to build fewer buildings using wood.

_____ Number of correct answers

Record your personal assessment of your work on the Critical Thinking Chart on page 58.

Summarizing and Paraphrasing

Follow the directions provided for questions 1 and 2. Put an X in the box next to the correct answer for the question 3.

1. Look for the important ideas and events in paragraphs 5 and 6. Summarize those paragraphs in one or two sentences.

_____

_____

_____

2. Complete the following one-sentence summary of the article using the lettered phrases from the phrase bank below. Write the letters on the lines.

> **Phrase Bank:**
> a. an explanation of how a firestorm works
> b. the Great Chicago Fire
> c. what happened to residents during the Peshtigo firestorm

The article "Firestorms" begins with _____, goes on to explain _____, and ends with _____.

3. Choose the best one-sentence paraphrase for the following sentence from the article: "Sawdust used in the streets to keep the dust down also burst into flames."

☐ a. People laid sawdust in the streets to reduce the dust in the air.

☐ b. Sawdust in the streets kept the fire from spreading.

☐ c. The fire ignited the sawdust that had been spread in the street to keep the dust down.

> _____ Number of correct answers
>
> Record your personal assessment of your work on the Critical Thinking Chart on page 58.

Critical Thinking

Follow the directions provided for questions 1, 2, and 3. Put an X in the box next to the correct answer for the other questions.

1. For each statement below, write O if it expresses an opinion or write F if it expresses a fact.

_____ a. The residents of Peshtigo should have had a volunteer fire department.

_____ b. In 1871 a fire destroyed more than two thousand acres in the city of Chicago.

_____ c. The upper part of a firestorm plume usually drifts away from the lower part.

2. Using what you know about the Peshtigo firestorm and what is told about the Great Chicago Fire in the article, name three ways the Peshtigo fire is similar to and three ways it is different from the Chicago fire. Cite the paragraph number(s) where you found details in the article to support your conclusions.

Similarities

_____

_____

Differences

_____

_____

3. Think about cause-effect relationships in the article. Fill in the blanks in the cause-effect chart, drawing from the letters below.

Cause	Effect
Brush fires often broke out in Peshtigo.	_____
The tops of firestorm plumes drift away from the fire's source.	_____
_____	All three people who jumped into the water tank died.

a. The fire heated up the water in the Peshtigo water tank.

b. Residents of Peshtigo were used to dealing with fires.

c. Rain from the firestorm plume rarely puts out the fire.

4. If you were a firefighter, how could you use the information in the article to prevent a firestorm from developing?

☐ a. If a fire starts, remove burnable material from the area as quickly as possible so that the fire runs out of fuel.

☐ b. Evacuate residents as quickly as possible.

☐ c. Hope for a windy day to keep the plume from developing.

_____ Number of correct answers

Record your personal assessment of your work on the Critical Thinking Chart on page 58.

Personal Response

What was most surprising or interesting to you about this article?

_____

_____

_____

Self-Assessment

I'm proud of my answer to question _____ in the _____ section because _____

_____

_____

Dowsing: Fact or Fiction?

Ray Burbank was having trouble finding an underground water pipe. So he asked a friend named Henry Gross for help. Gross took a Y-shaped twig and held it in his hands. Then he walked back and forth over the ground. "The pipe's right here," Gross said at last, marking the spot with a wooden stake.

2   Meanwhile, the water company had sent its own men to find the pipe. When the men saw Gross with the twig, they broke out laughing. Still, even though they used fancy

For more than 300 years, people have been using dowsing rods to find things hidden underground, such as metal objects, ancient relics, and—most importantly—water. Today, scientists are trying to find out if dowsing really works and, if so, how.

machines, they couldn't find the pipe. The next day, Ray Burbank dug up the spot Gross had marked. Sure enough, there was the water pipe.

3   Gross found the pipe by using the age-old art of dowsing. Dowsers claim they can find water and other hidden things under the earth. They simply walk over the ground while holding a forked stick or rod. Suddenly, they say, the stick or rod will tremble in the dowser's hands. It will point down toward what is hidden below the ground. When asked what makes the stick move, many dowsers shrug. "I don't know how it works," they say. "It just does."

4   Henry Gross is not the only dowser to amaze his neighbors. An old Vermont farmer named Milford Preston was famous for picking the best place to drill for water. One day a friend challenged Preston to a test. The friend dumped five piles of sand behind his barn. He told Preston he had hidden a quarter in one of the piles. In truth, the friend was trying to trick Preston. He had actually hidden quarters in two different piles.

5   Preston picked up a forked stick and went to work. He stopped over the second pile. He could tell a quarter was buried there. But to be sure, Preston checked the other piles. He knew right away that there was another quarter in the fifth pile. "You're not as tricky as you thought you were!" Preston smirked.

6   Dowsing goes back at least to the 16th century. That's when the first written account of it appeared in Germany. In those days, dowsing was used to find precious metals. The practice spread throughout Europe and, later, the United States. People in Asia and Africa also began to practice dowsing. Over time, dowsers have expanded their claims. Today they still say they can find water, pipelines, and metals. But they also say they can locate buried treasure. They claim they can find ancient relics, land mines, and dead bodies. Some dowsers even insist they can find objects just by swinging a chain over a map. The chain, they say, will pull their hand toward the right spot.

7   Some of today's dowsers have a pretty good record of success. One of the very best dowsers is Hans Schröter. Schröter has spent a lot of time in Sri Lanka. He has picked sites for hundreds of wells

there. In fact, he has chosen 691 spots. Only 27 of these have failed to yield water.

8   Still, the question remains: How do dowsers do it? What could make a stick suddenly bend down toward something far underground? Is there some force in nature at work? Some people think there is. They believe each hidden object must send out some kind of mysterious wave. Water, too, must send out waves. Dowsers, then, would be people sensitive enough to pick up these waves.

9   Few scientists believe in such unseen waves. Some say that dowsers' success stories are just a matter of luck. Others have a different theory. It's not the stick that helps a dowser, they say. It's the dowser's own knowledge of the land. Most dowsers are not geologists. They have no formal training in earth science. Still, they often know the land they are walking very well. So they might pick up clues without even realizing it. They might see that underground water changes the look of the soil in a certain area. The shape of the ground might offer hints. So, too, might the presence of certain plants or grasses. Geologist Jay Lehr says that experienced dowsers are often experts in picking up such clues. He says dowsers always "have an understanding, whether they're aware of it or not, of various surface clues."

10   Still, a few experts have decided that dowsing is for real. One is the German scientist Hans-Dieter Betz. In 1995 Betz wrote a report on dowsing. In it, he declared that good dowsers can indeed detect water below the ground. Betz is respected in his field. His report has caused other scientists to take a second look at dowsing. So far, though, most are not convinced.

11   So that puts us back where we started. Is dowsing fact or fiction? Tests have shown that it does work. But all of these tests, including ones done by Betz, have been challenged. Critics of dowsing say that every test has been flawed in one way or another. So dowsing remains an open question. Most scientists still reject it. But many people around the world practice it. Can they all be wrong?

If you have been timed while reading this article, enter your reading time below. Then turn to the Words-per-Minute Table on page 55 and look up your reading speed (words per minute). Enter your reading speed on the graph on page 56.

Reading Time: Lesson 5

_____ : _____
Minutes   Seconds

A Finding the Main Idea

One statement below expresses the main idea of the article. One statement is too general, or too broad. The other statement explains only part of the article; it is too narrow. Label the statements using the following key:

M—Main Idea   **B—Too Broad**   **N—Too Narrow**

_____ 1. Dowsers use a forked stick or rod that trembles when it is placed over a buried object.

_____ 2. Dowsing is a good way to find hidden objects.

_____ 3. The dowsing method of finding buried objects seems to be a combination of art, skill, and luck.

_____ Score 15 points for a correct M answer.

_____ Score 5 points for each correct B or N answer.

_____ **Total Score:** Finding the Main Idea

B Recalling Facts

How well do you remember the facts in the article? Put an X in the box next to the answer that correctly completes each statement about the article.

1. When the water company men saw the dowser whom Ray Burbank had hired, they
   - ☐ a. made him leave the land.
   - ☐ b. asked him for help.
   - ☐ c. laughed at him.

2. Dowsers find water and hidden objects by
   - ☐ a. walking over ground with a forked stick.
   - ☐ b. listening to the sound a forked stick makes.
   - ☐ c. closing their eyes and thinking hard.

3. The first written account of dowsing came from
   - ☐ a. Africa.
   - ☐ b. Mexico.
   - ☐ c. Germany.

4. Some dowsers say that when they want to find something, a chain swung over a map can
   - ☐ a. make them dizzy.
   - ☐ b. pull their hand toward the right spot.
   - ☐ c. help them think better.

5. When the forked stick is held over a buried object, the stick
   - ☐ a. bends down toward the ground.
   - ☐ b. jumps out of the dowser's hand.
   - ☐ c. becomes hot in the dowser's hand.

Score 5 points for each correct answer.

_____ **Total Score:** Recalling Facts

C | Making Inferences

When you combine your own experience and information from a text to draw a conclusion that is not directly stated in that text, you are making an inference. Below are five statements that may or may not be inferences based on information in the article. Label the statements using the following key:

C—Correct Inference   F—Faulty Inference

_____ 1. One of the advantages of dowsing is that it can be done with cheap tools.

_____ 2. Only men can become dowsers.

_____ 3. The need for wells in Sri Lanka is great.

_____ 4. If scientists say they don't believe in a practice such as dowsing, everyone around the world gives it up.

_____ 5. Most dowsers have studied about rocks and the earth in college.

Score 5 points for each correct answer.

_____ **Total Score:** Making Inferences

D | Using Words Precisely

Each numbered sentence below contains an underlined word or phrase from the article. Following the sentence are three definitions. One definition is closest to the meaning of the underlined word. One definition is opposite or nearly opposite. Label those two definitions using the following key; do not label the remaining definition.

C—Closest   O—Opposite or Nearly Opposite

1. Only 27 of these have failed to <u>yield</u> water.

_____ a. hold back

_____ b. spray

_____ c. give up

2. Suddenly, they say, the stick or rod will <u>tremble</u> in their hands.

_____ a. shake

_____ b. remain steady

_____ c. twist

3. In those days, dowsing was used to find <u>precious</u> metals.

_____ a. beautiful

_____ b. valuable

_____ c. worthless

4. Some dowsers even <u>insist</u> they can find objects just by swinging a chain over a map.

_____ a. deny

_____ b. believe

_____ c. say firmly

5. Critics of dowsing say that every test has been <u>flawed</u> in one way or another.

_____ a. perfect

_____ b. imperfect

_____ c. hard to believe

_____ Score 3 points for each correct C answer.

_____ Score 2 points for each correct O answer.

_____ **Total Score:** Using Words Precisely

Enter the four total scores in the spaces below, and add them together to find your Reading Comprehension Score. Then record your score on the graph on page 57.

Score	Question Type	Lesson 5
_____	Finding the Main Idea	
_____	Recalling Facts	
_____	Making Inferences	
_____	Using Words Precisely	
_____	**Reading Comprehension Score**	

Author's Approach

Put an X in the box next to the correct answer.

1. What do the authors mean by the statement "Dowsing goes back at least to the 16th century"?

☐ a. Dowsing may have worked in the 16th century, but it probably doesn't work now.

☐ b. Since dowsing is so old, no one can take it seriously today.

☐ c. Since dowsing has survived so long, it is possible that it may actually work.

2. Judging by statements from the article, you can conclude that the authors want the reader to think that dowsing

☐ a. is the best way to find underground water.

☐ b. may work at times, but no one knows how.

☐ c. is a trick that crooks play on unsuspecting victims.

3. Dowsers claim that they feel their dowsing sticks tremble when they are over water. Choose the statement below that best explains how the authors address the opposing point of view in the article.

☐ a. The authors point out that dowsers may unconsciously use their knowledge of the land, rather than movements of the dowsing stick, to find water.

☐ b. The authors note that even dowsers don't know how dowsing works.

☐ c. The authors tell about one dowser who has an excellent record in finding underground water.

_____ Number of correct answers

Record your personal assessment of your work on the Critical Thinking Chart on page 58.

Summarizing and Paraphrasing

Follow the directions provided for question 1. Put an X in the box next to the correct answer for question 2.

1. Reread paragraph 7 in the article. Below, write a summary of the paragraph in no more than 25 words.

_____

_____

_____

_____

Reread your summary and decide whether it covers the important ideas in the paragraph. Next, decide how to shorten the summary to 15 words or less without leaving out any essential information. Write this summary below.

_____

_____

_____

2. Read the statement from the article below. Then read the paraphrase of that statement. Choose the reason that best tells why the paraphrase does not say the same thing as the statement.

Statement: Although dowsing was first used as a way to find precious metals, over the centuries people have used it to find many buried items.

Paraphrase: When dowsing began, people used it mostly to locate precious metals, but now dowsers say they can find ancient relics, land mines, dead bodies, water, and pipelines, in addition to metals.

☐ a. Paraphrase says too much.

☐ b. Paraphrase doesn't say enough.

☐ c. Paraphrase doesn't agree with the statement.

_____ Number of correct answers

Record your personal assessment of your work on the Critical Thinking Chart on page 58.

Critical Thinking

Put an X in the box next to the correct answer for questions 1, 2, and 5. Follow the directions provided for the other questions.

1. Which of the following statements from the article is an opinion rather than a fact?

☐ a. Some of today's dowsers have a pretty good record of success.

☐ b. Most dowsers are not geologists.

☐ c. Few scientists believe in such unseen waves.

2. Considering Hans Schröter's actions as told in this article, you can predict that

☐ a. he would be embarrassed to talk about his work.

☐ b. many people will ask him for help in finding underground water.

☐ c. his clients will probably not be happy with his work.

3. Choose from the letters below to correctly complete the following statement. Write the letters on the lines.

On the positive side, _____, but on the negative side, _____.

a. dowsing actually works sometimes

b. believing you can find water with a stick seems silly to many people

c. dowsing began in the 16th century

4. Reread paragraph 9. Then choose from the letters below to correctly complete the following statement. Write the letters on the lines.

According to paragraph 9, some scientists say that _____ because _____.

a. dowsers have no formal training in earth science

b. dowsers can pick up details about whether there is underground water from the look of the soil or the type of plants growing there

c. dowsers sometimes can find underground water

5. What did you have to do to answer question 3?

☐ a. find an opinion (what someone thinks about something)

☐ b. find a description (how something looks)

☐ c. find a contrast (how things are different)

_____ Number of correct answers

Record your personal assessment of your work on the Critical Thinking Chart on page 58.

Personal Response

I wonder why _____

_____

_____

Self-Assessment

One of the things I did best when reading this article was _____

_____

_____

I believe I did this well because _____

_____

_____

Compare and Contrast

Think about the articles you have read in Unit One. Pick three articles about ideas that you find difficult to believe. Write the titles of those articles in the first column of the chart below. Use information you learned from the articles to fill in the empy boxes in the chart.

Title	Which ideas from the article are hard to believe?	Which person or persons believe these ideas?	How have believers explained or proved their theories?

The idea that I had the most trouble believing was _____. I found it hard to believe because _____

_____

_____

Words-per-Minute Table

Unit One

Directions: If you were timed while reading an article, refer to the Reading Time you recorded in the box at the end of the article. Use this Words-per-Minute Table to determine your reading speed for that article. Then plot your reading speed on the graph on page 56.

Lesson / No. of Words	Sample 630	1 855	2 921	3 1,017	4 901	5 847	Seconds
1:30	420	570	614	678	601	565	90
1:40	378	513	553	610	541	508	100
1:50	344	466	502	555	491	462	110
2:00	315	428	461	509	451	424	120
2:10	291	395	425	469	416	391	130
2:20	270	366	395	436	386	363	140
2:30	252	342	368	407	360	339	150
2:40	236	321	345	381	338	318	160
2:50	222	302	325	359	318	299	170
3:00	210	285	307	339	300	282	180
3:10	199	270	291	321	285	267	190
3:20	189	257	276	305	270	254	200
3:30	180	244	263	291	257	242	210
3:40	172	233	251	277	246	231	220
3:50	164	223	240	265	235	221	230
4:00	158	214	230	254	225	212	240
4:10	151	205	221	244	216	203	250
4:20	145	197	213	235	208	195	260
4:30	140	190	205	226	200	188	270
4:40	135	183	197	218	193	182	280
4:50	130	177	191	210	186	175	290
5:00	126	171	184	203	180	169	300
5:10	122	165	178	197	174	164	310
5:20	118	160	173	191	169	159	320
5:30	115	155	167	185	164	154	330
5:40	111	151	163	179	159	149	340
5:50	108	147	158	174	154	145	350
6:00	105	143	154	170	150	141	360
6:10	102	139	149	165	146	137	370
6:20	99	135	145	161	142	134	380
6:30	97	132	142	156	139	130	390
6:40	95	128	138	153	135	127	400
6:50	92	125	135	149	132	124	410
7:00	90	122	132	145	129	121	420
7:10	88	119	129	142	126	118	430
7:20	86	117	126	139	123	116	440
7:30	84	114	123	136	120	113	450
7:40	82	112	120	133	118	110	460
7:50	80	109	118	130	115	108	470
8:00	79	107	115	127	113	106	480

Minutes and Seconds

Plotting Your Progress: Reading Speed

Unit One

Directions: If you were timed while reading an article, write your words-per-minute rate for that article in the box under the number of the lesson. Then plot your reading speed on the graph by putting a small X on the line directly above the number of the lesson, across from the number of words per minute you read. As you mark your speed for each lesson, graph your progress by drawing a line to connect the X's.

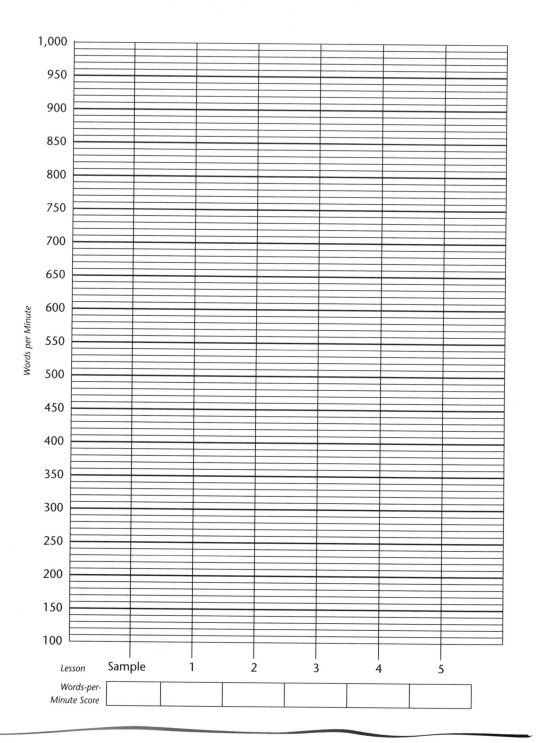

Words per Minute

Lesson	Sample	1	2	3	4	5
Words-per-Minute Score						

Plotting Your Progress: Reading Comprehension

Unit One

Directions: Write your Reading Comprehension Score for each lesson in the box under the number of the lesson. Then plot your score on the graph by putting a small X on the line directly above the number of the lesson and across from the score you earned. As you mark your score for each lesson, graph your progress by drawing a line to connect the X's.

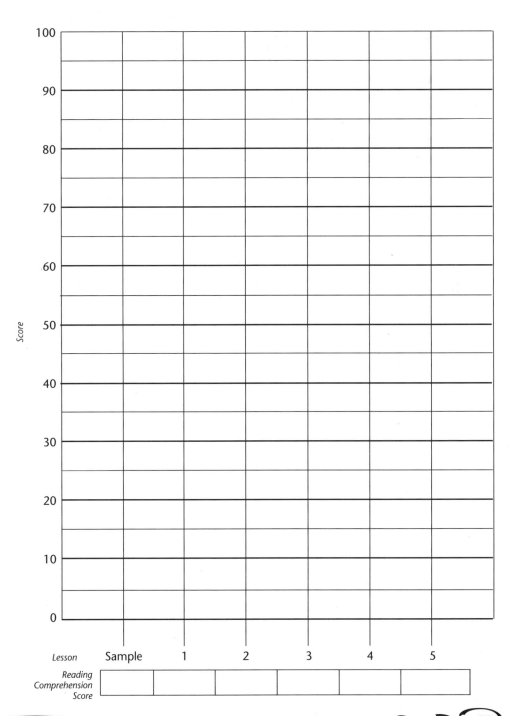

Lesson	Sample	1	2	3	4	5
Reading Comprehension Score						

Plotting Your Progress: Critical Thinking

Unit One

Directions: Work with your teacher to evaluate your responses to the Critical Thinking questions for each lesson. Then fill in the appropriate spaces in the chart below. For each lesson and each type of Critical Thinking question, do the following: Mark a minus sign (–) in the box to indicate areas in which you feel you could improve. Mark a plus sign (+) to indicate areas in which you feel you did well. Mark a minus-slash-plus sign (–/+) to indicate areas in which you had mixed success. Then write any comments you have about your performance, including ideas for improvement.

Lesson	Author's Approach		Summarizing and Paraphrasing		Critical Thinking	
Sample						
1						
2						
3						
4						
5						

UNIT TWO

Traveling Through Time

Imagine being able to travel 200 years into the future. Or think about taking a journey far back into the past. Time travel has long been a dream for many people. But is it just a dream? Until recently, everyone thought so. It was fun to ponder, scientists said, but it wasn't really possible. Now, some scientists are changing their minds. They say that maybe, just maybe, time travel is possible.

2   Think about time for a minute. What is it, really? You can watch the second hand on a clock move around

This strange vehicle carries the hero of the movie The Time Machine *forward in time. H. G. Wells wrote the novel from which the movie was based in 1895. But the idea of time travel has had a grip on our imaginations for centuries.*

the dial. If you watch it long enough, you'll see the minute hand move. And if you wait even longer, you'll notice that the hour hand also moves. The clock on the wall is one measure of time. But it is not the only measure.

3   A great scientist named Albert Einstein showed that time has many measures. As a young man, Einstein thought a lot about light and time. One day he had a thought that no one had ever had before. Einstein wondered what a clock would look like if he were riding away from it on a beam of light. He guessed that the clock would appear to stand still. In other words, time would stand still!

4   Why did Einstein make that guess? Imagine that a clock reads exactly 2 P.M. You can see that because light shining off the clock shows the position of the hands. The light travels to your eye and your brain reads, "2 P.M." A second later, the hand on the clock moves to one second after 2 P.M. Light is still bouncing off the clock. So another beam of light carries a new message to your eye. Now your brain reads, "one second after 2:00 P.M." Beams of light travel so fast that you can read each

message instantly. But imagine riding on the beam of light that carries the "2 P.M." message. The other beam of light—the one carrying the message "one second after 2 P.M."—would never catch up with you. So for you, the clock would always read "2 P.M."

5   Using experiments, Einstein proved his guess was right. He confirmed that speed slows down the passage of time. In that sense, everyone has already done at least a tiny bit of time traveling. You have done it each time you have ridden in a car or plane. Such time travel, however, is far too slight to notice.

6   Now think like Einstein. Suppose you go very, very fast. In fact, you go almost the speed of light. (Light travels at about 186,000 miles per second! That's more than a million times faster than a jet plane!) At that speed, you'd find that time really does slow down. Messages from other beams of light would catch up with you, but only after a long chase.

7   Because speed slows down time, you would age slowly as you zip through space. Meanwhile, back on Earth, time would pass as it always does. While you'd be getting five years older, people

on Earth might be getting 205 years older. If you return to Earth after your five years, you would find you had traveled 200 years into the future!

8 Such time travel is not feasible yet. The fastest spaceships can go only a few thousand miles an hour. We haven't found a way to go any faster. In theory, however, there is a way we could do it. We could use what is called a black hole. A black hole, if it really exists, is a gigantic star that has used up all its fuel. It has collapsed into itself, becoming very small. The gravitational pull from a black hole would be immense. It would be so great, in fact, that everything passing by it—even light beams—would get sucked in. Things would get trapped in a wild funnel that looks a bit like a tornado. The winds in this funnel would be close to the speed of light.

9 If a spaceship could approach the funnel at just the right angle, the black hole might act as a slingshot. It could whip the spaceship around and send it flying back out through space at a super-high speed. (Of course, the pilot would have to be very careful. He or she could not fly too close to the black hole. Otherwise, the whole spaceship would get pulled in and compressed to less than the size of a grain of sand!)

10 Now imagine that you want to travel back into the past. That would be even harder to do. You would have to catch up with light beams carrying messages from long ago. To do that, you'd have to travel faster than the speed of light. That is not possible. Nothing can go faster than a light beam. Still, some scientists think there's a way to get around that problem. They suggest taking a shortcut through space. That way, a traveler might be able to catch up with some old beams of light. Scientists have a picture in their minds of what this kind of shortcut would look like. They have even given it a name. They call it a "wormhole." No one knows if wormholes exist. But if they do, travelers might someday use them to jump back in time.

11 Before you get too excited about traveling to the past, think about some of the questions it would raise. Suppose you traveled back to April 14, 1865. That was the day President Abraham Lincoln was shot. Could you prevent the assassination? Suppose you did. How would that change the course of American history?

12 Scientists often put the questions in personal terms. Suppose you time-travel back 60 years, to the days when your grandmother is a young woman. Your mother has not yet been born. If you somehow stop your grandmother from meeting your grandfather, where does that leave you? Now your mother won't be born. Does this mean you will cease to exist?

13 People love to fantasize about time travel. The question is this: can we really find a way to do it? Will it remain just a dream, carried out only in books or at the movies? Or will we someday be able to fly off into the future and back into the past? Only time will tell.

A Finding the Main Idea

One statement below expresses the main idea of the article. One statement is too general, or too broad. The other statement explains only part of the article; it is too narrow. Label the statements using the following key:

M—Main Idea   **B—Too Broad**   **N—Too Narrow**

_____ 1. Some scientists have explored the idea of time travel and believe that it may be possible one day.

_____ 2. Scientists are fascinated by the idea of time travel.

_____ 3. Albert Einstein proved that speed slows down the passage of time.

_____ Score 15 points for a correct M answer.

_____ Score 5 points for each correct B or N answer.

_____ **Total Score:** Finding the Main Idea

B Recalling Facts

How well do you remember the facts in the article? Put an X in the box next to the answer that correctly completes each statement about the article.

1. Light travels at the speed of
   - ☐ a. 186,000 feet per second.
   - ☐ b. 186,000 miles per hour.
   - ☐ c. 186,000 miles per second.

2. A black hole is a star that
   - ☐ a. has used up all its fuel.
   - ☐ b. is getting ready to explode.
   - ☐ c. moves faster than the speed of light.

3. Near a black hole, a spaceship could
   - ☐ a. explode.
   - ☐ b. get pulled in and compressed.
   - ☐ c. lose speed and stop moving.

4. To catch up with light beams carrying messages from long ago, you would need to travel
   - ☐ a. the speed of light.
   - ☐ b. the speed of sound.
   - ☐ c. faster than the speed of light.

5. A shortcut through space is sometimes called a
   - ☐ a. funnel.
   - ☐ b. wormhole.
   - ☐ c. slingshot.

Score 5 points for each correct answer.

_____ **Total Score:** Recalling Facts

C | Making Inferences

When you combine your own experience and information from a text to draw a conclusion that is not directly stated in that text, you are making an inference. Below are five statements that may or may not be inferences based on information in the article. Label the statements using the following key:

C—Correct Inference   **F—Faulty Inference**

_____ 1. Most scientists ignore the work of Albert Einstein.

_____ 2. Only the finest pilots should fly their ships near black holes.

_____ 3. Someday spaceships will go faster than the speed of light.

_____ 4. If a mother began to travel at almost the speed of light, she could become younger than her daughter who stayed on Earth.

_____ 5. In theory, changing past events would probably have no effect on the present or the future.

Score 5 points for each correct answer.

_____ **Total Score:** Making Inferences

D | Using Words Precisely

Each numbered sentence below contains an underlined word or phrase from the article. Following the sentence are three definitions. One definition is closest to the meaning of the underlined word. One definition is opposite or nearly opposite. Label those two definitions using the following key; do not label the remaining definition.

C—Closest   **O—Opposite or Nearly Opposite**

1. Beams of light travel so fast that you can read each message <u>instantly</u>.

_____ a. slowly

_____ b. immediately

_____ c. clearly

2. Does that mean that you <u>cease</u> to exist?

_____ a. stop

_____ b. begin

_____ c. want

3. He <u>confirmed</u> that speed slows down the passage of time.

_____ a. guessed

_____ b. disproved

_____ c. proved

4. Such time travel is not <u>feasible</u> yet.

_____ a. possible

_____ b. impossible

_____ c. planned

5. The gravitational pull from a black hole would be <u>immense</u>.

_____ a. collapsed

_____ b. huge

_____ c. small

_____ Score 3 points for each correct C answer.

_____ Score 2 points for each correct O answer.

_____ **Total Score:** Using Words Precisely

Enter the four total scores in the spaces below, and add them together to find your Reading Comprehension Score. Then record your score on the graph on page 103.

Score	Question Type	Lesson 6
_____	Finding the Main Idea	
_____	Recalling Facts	
_____	Making Inferences	
_____	Using Words Precisely	
_____	**Reading Comprehension Score**	

Author's Approach

Put an X in the box next to the correct answer.

1. What is the authors' purpose in writing "Traveling Through Time"?

☐ a. to express an opinion about time travel

☐ b. to inform the reader about theories relating to time travel

☐ c. to compare travel through time and travel though space

2. Which of the following statements from the article best describes a black hole?

☐ a. a gigantic star that has used up all its fuel

☐ b. a shortcut through space

☐ c. light beams carrying messages from long ago

3. From the statements below, choose those that you believe the authors would agree with.

☐ a. Albert Einstein was a creative thinker and a careful scientist.

☐ b. Scientists are very close to finding a way for the average person to travel through time.

☐ c. It would be easier to travel to the future than to travel to the past.

4. What do the authors imply by saying "Scientists have a picture in their minds of what this kind of shortcut would look like"?

☐ a. If a thing can't be observed or measured, scientists are not interested in it.

☐ b. Science deals only with facts, not with unproven ideas.

☐ c. Scientists often use their imaginations to come up with new theories.

_____ Number of correct answers

Record your personal assessment of your work on the Critical Thinking Chart on page 104.

Summarizing and Paraphrasing

Follow the directions provided for questions 1 and 2. Put an X in the box next to the correct answer for question 3.

1. Complete the following one-sentence summary of the article using the lettered phrases from the phrase bank below. Write the letters on the lines.

> **Phrase Bank:**
> a. Albert Einstein's thoughts on time travel
> b. how time travel could affect history
> c. how black holes and wormholes could be used for time travel

The article "Traveling Through Time" begins with _____, goes on to explain _____, and ends with _____.

2. Reread paragraph 9 in the article. Below, write a summary of the paragraph in no more than 25 words.

_____

_____

_____

Reread your summary and decide whether it covers the important ideas in the paragraph. Next, decide how to shorten the summary to 15 words or less without leaving out any essential information. Write this summary below.

_____

_____

_____

3. Choose the best one-sentence paraphrase for the following sentence from the article: "Now imagine that you want to travel back into the past. . . . You would have to catch up with light beams carrying messages from long ago."

☐ a. Traveling back into the past would require the traveler to catch up with light beams of long ago.

☐ b. To catch up with old light beams, you would need to travel to the past.

☐ c. Light beams carrying messages from the past will one day help people travel back in time.

_____ Number of correct answers

Record your personal assessment of your work on the Critical Thinking Chart on page 104.

Critical Thinking

Follow the directions provided for questions 1 and 4. Put an X in the box next to the correct answer for the other questions.

1. For each statement below, write *O* if it expresses an opinion or write *F* if it expresses a fact.

_____ a. The idea of traveling through time is exciting.

_____ b. Albert Einstein was the greatest scientist ever.

_____ c. Light travels at the speed of 186,000 miles per second.

2. From the article, you can predict that if you traveled at almost the speed of light for 10 years and then returned to Earth, people there would be

☐ a. more than 10 years older.

☐ b. fewer than 10 years older.

☐ c. exactly 10 years older.

3. What did Einstein think the effect of traveling at the speed of light would be?

☐ a. The traveler would die.

☐ b. To the traveler, time would appear to speed up.

☐ c. To the traveler, time would appear to stand still.

4. In which paragraph did you find your information or details to answer question 2? _____

_____ Number of correct answers

Record your personal assessment of your work on the Critical Thinking Chart on page 104.

Personal Response

Begin the first 5–8 sentences of your own article about an imaginary trip through time.

_____

_____

_____

_____

Self-Assessment

Which concepts or ideas from the article were difficult to understand?

_____

_____

_____

Which were easy?

_____

_____

_____

A Silent Killer

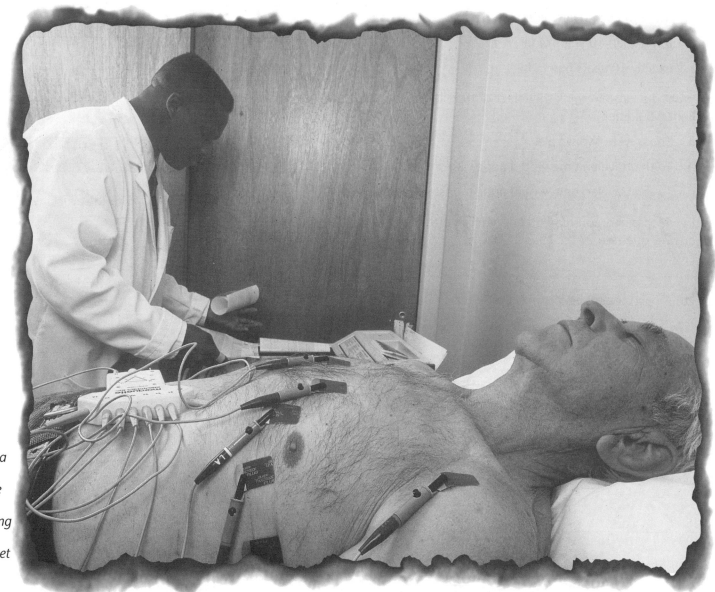

This man is having his heart tested for a rare disease that causes people to die suddenly in their sleep. It's called Long QT syndrome, and most people who get it never find out.

In 1979 Doris Goldman got a phone call she would never forget. It came late at night. "Are you Jack Toran's mother?" asked the caller.

2   "Is he OK?"

3   "Didn't anyone call you?" said the voice. "This is the coroner calling from Jackson Hole, Wyoming."

4   "Was he in an accident?"

5   "No. He died peacefully in his sleep."

6   The news broke Goldman's heart. She wondered how it was possible. Jack was a fine athlete. The 20-year-old had never been seriously ill. The day he died, Jack had been hiking with friends in the Grand Tetons. The doctors said his death must have been caused by the high altitude. That didn't make sense to Goldman. Thousands of other people climb in these mountains and don't die. Something else was at work here. But what?

7   Elsewhere, other young people were dying in mysterious ways. A seven-year-old boy died in his sleep. A 23-year-old died taking a nap. A 30-year-old dropped dead as she walked to get a drink of water after playing soccer. A 19-year-old nearly drowned while swimming laps in a shallow pool. A few hours later, she did die.

8   That was just the tip of the iceberg. About four thousand young people died every year for no apparent reason. Weirdly, they seemed to be in fine shape until the moment they died. Some were even top athletes. What was going on? Was there a link to tie them together? If so, what was it? For a long time, no one had an answer.

9   Doris Goldman was as stymied as anyone else. Jack's friends told her he had fainted earlier that week. This meant nothing to Goldman at the time. Most of the time, fainting does not signify serious health problems. The people recover and go on with their lives.

10   But a year later Goldman got a call from her daughter Sharon. Sharon had just had a fainting spell. Thinking back to Jack, Sharon and her mother grew nervous. Goldman began to wonder if the fainting spells had a common cause. She wondered if her children had been born with some unknown heart condition. A doctor tested Sharon's heart. The beat was slow and irregular. But that was not uncommon for a young athlete like Sharon. She was a top water-skier and runner. Sharon also had a problem with a valve in her heart. But the doctor said that was not a threat to her health.

11   In 1981 Goldman got yet another call she would never forget. Sharon had fainted while walking across her bedroom. Her heart had stopped beating. For a few minutes her brain received no oxygen. Sharon did not die, but she fell into a coma. She stayed unconscious for two weeks.

12   The lack of oxygen damaged Sharon's brain. She had to stay in the hospital for several months. After that she spent six years fighting to regain her health and strength. At last she did. It seemed as if all that hard work had paid off. Sharon took a drug to control her heartbeat. Later, she got married. In 1991 she had a baby named Jacob. It seemed that Sharon's life was back to normal.

13 Sadly, Sharon died in her sleep a few months later. "It was too much to have her come so far and then lose her," said Doris Goldman. The heart drug Sharon had been using was the right one. But her doctor had prescribed a dose that was too small.

14 There was good news, however. Doctors at the University of Utah had zeroed in on the cause of death. It was something called Long QT syndrome. The name comes from the long time between two beats *(Q and T)* in a defective heart. Long QT makes the heart beat wildly at times. At other times, it makes the heart stop.

15 Some people, such as Jack and Sharon, are born with it. But a person can acquire Long QT by taking the wrong medicine. Also, doctors have found out why only young people die from Long QT. In this case, it pays to be old. As people age, their hearts start to beat more regularly. So, if Long QT does not kill a person in youth, chances are it won't ever kill him or her.

16 Few people have ever heard of Long QT syndrome. It takes a heart test called an EKG to detect this rare defect. Even then, a doctor has to be looking for it. Long QT is very easy to miss. That is why so many young people died before researchers put the pieces of the puzzle together.

17 Even now, young people still die. That's because most of them don't get an EKG. After all, their hearts are supposed to be strong. And, in the vast majority of cases, they are. So doctors may think it is unnecessary to test them. Even those who are tested can slip through without having the defect caught. "Doctors miss it all the time," said one woman who lost her 19-year-old son to Long QT.

18 Most people who die from Long QT never know what hit them. There may be some warning signs. Fainting may mean that something is wrong. Feeling light in the head can be a danger signal. But some people have no warning at all. One day they just drop dead. Their hearts are like time bombs waiting to go off. The fatal trigger can be exercise such as swimming or running. Or it can be a shock as simple as a surprise doorbell ring. One woman died when a two-year-old darted past her down an aisle in church. Death can even be triggered by the stress of a bad dream.

19 Doris Goldman's hunch was right. Jack and Sharon were born with Long QT. She checked the heart records of her family back as far as she could. She discovered that 21 members of her family had Long QT. She had it herself. So, too, did her one living daughter, Nancy. Sharon's young son, Jacob, was also born with it. But, luckily, they now knew it. With the right treatment, Jacob should be OK.

20 Goldman started a campaign to teach victims as well as doctors about Long QT. She called the heart defect "a silent killer." But it doesn't have to be a killer. While there is no cure, there are drugs to treat it. So, if someone has a family history of sudden death, he or she should get an EKG. It could save a life.

21 Goldman's campaign has helped give meaning to the deaths of Jack and Sharon. "I stay sane because I can help someone else," she once said. "No other family should have to go through what we've been through. The only way for me to go on was to take a tragedy and turn it into a mission."

If you have been timed while reading this article, enter your reading time below. Then turn to the Words-per-Minute Table on page 101 and look up your reading speed (words per minute). Enter your reading speed on the graph on page 102.

Reading Time: Lesson 7

———— : ————

Minutes   Seconds

A Finding the Main Idea

One statement below expresses the main idea of the article. One statement is too general, or too broad. The other statement explains only part of the article; it is too narrow. Label the statements using the following key:

M—Main Idea   **B—Too Broad**   **N—Too Narrow**

_____ 1. Young people who have Long QT syndrome, which causes the heart to beat very fast or very slowly, sometimes die quite suddenly. Only now are scientists beginning to understand and treat the disease.

_____ 2. Jack Goldman was a fine athlete who had just completed a day of hiking in the Grand Tetons when he died in his sleep. The cause was Long QT syndrome.

_____ 3. Long QT can kill young, vigorous people and leave their loved ones saddened and surprised.

_____ Score 15 points for a correct M answer.

_____ Score 5 points for each correct B or N answer.

_____ **Total Score:** Finding the Main Idea

B Recalling Facts

How well do you remember the facts in the article? Put an X in the box next to the answer that correctly completes each statement about the article.

1. One warning sign that a person may have Long QT is
   ☐ a. occasional fainting spells.
   ☐ b. a severe headache.
   ☐ c. a rash.

2. Sharon's brain was damaged by
   ☐ a. an auto accident.
   ☐ b. a bad fall.
   ☐ c. a lack of oxygen.

3. Long QT kills its victims by
   ☐ a. giving them strokes.
   ☐ b. making their hearts beat wildly or stop suddenly.
   ☐ c. bursting the victims' blood vessels.

4. Doctors can detect Long QT using
   ☐ a. a stethoscope.
   ☐ b. a test called an EKG.
   ☐ c. an X ray.

5. Those who are most in danger of dying of Long QT are
   ☐ a. young people.
   ☐ b. middle-aged people.
   ☐ c. people over the age of 70.

Score 5 points for each correct answer.

_____ **Total Score:** Recalling Facts

C Making Inferences

When you combine your own experience with information from a text to draw a conclusion that is not directly stated in that text, you are making an inference. Below are five statements that may or may not be inferences based on information in the article. Label the statements using the following key:

C—Correct Inference   F—Faulty Inference

_____ 1. Jack Goldman probably knew he was dying when he went to bed that last night.

_____ 2. Most people who die at a young age are killed by Long QT.

_____ 3. Doris Goldman's crusade to inform people about Long QT has probably saved lives.

_____ 4. Young people who have fainted should be given EKG tests.

_____ 5. Doctors can often help you more if they know about your family's health history.

Score 5 points for each correct answer.

_____ **Total Score:** Making Inferences

D Using Words Precisely

Each numbered sentence below contains an underlined word or phrase from the article. Following the sentence are three definitions. One definition is closest to the meaning of the underlined word. One definition is opposite or nearly opposite. Label those two definitions using the following key; do not label the remaining definition.

C—Closest   O—Opposite or Nearly Opposite

1. About four thousand young people died every year for no <u>apparent</u> reason.

_____ a. obvious

_____ b. hard to detect

_____ c. famous

2. Doris Goldman was as <u>stymied</u> as anyone else.

_____ a. careful and thrifty

_____ b. puzzled and frustrated

_____ c. certain and peaceful

3. But her doctor had <u>prescribed</u> a dose that was too small.

_____ a. forbidden the use of

_____ b. invented

_____ c. ordered the use of

4. But a person can <u>acquire</u> Long QT by taking the wrong medicine.

_____ a. lose

_____ b. get

_____ c. fear

5. After all, their hearts are supposed to be strong. And, in the vast <u>majority</u> of cases, they are.

_____ a. treatment

_____ b. smaller number

_____ c. greater number

_____ Score 3 points for each correct C answer.

_____ Score 2 points for each correct O answer.

_____ **Total Score:** Using Words Precisely

Enter the four total scores in the spaces below, and add them together to find your Reading Comprehension Score. Then record your score on the graph on page 103.

Score	Question Type	Lesson 7
_____	Finding the Main Idea	
_____	Recalling Facts	
_____	Making Inferences	
_____	Using Words Precisely	
_____	**Reading Comprehension Score**	

Author's Approach

Put an X in the box next to the correct answer.

1. What is the authors' purpose in writing "A Silent Killer"?

☐ a. to inform the reader about a serious but treatable health problem

☐ b. to describe situations in which young people died unexpectedly

☐ c. to convey a mood of sadness

2. Which of the following statements from the article best describes the reason why Doris Goldman was so surprised that her son had died?

☐ a. Doctors said his death must have been caused by the high altitude.

☐ b. Jack's friends told her he had fainted earlier that week.

☐ c. The 20-year-old had never been seriously ill.

3. From the statements below, choose those that you believe the authors would agree with.

☐ a. Doctors should give EKG tests to more young people to check them for Long QT.

☐ b. Many Long QT deaths can be prevented with proper treatment.

☐ c. Most young people have Long QT but don't know it.

4. In this article, "Their hearts are like time bombs waiting to go off" means

☐ a. their hearts may explode in their chests.

☐ b. their hearts could give them trouble at any time without warning.

☐ c. these people always feel nervous.

_____ Number of correct answers

Record your personal assessment of your work on the Critical Thinking Chart on page 104.

Summarizing and Paraphrasing

Follow the directions provided for question 1. Put an X in the box next to the correct answer for question 2.

1. Reread paragraph 20 in the article. Below, write a summary of the paragraph in no more than 25 words.

_____

_____

_____

_____

Reread your summary and decide whether it covers the important ideas in the paragraph. Next, decide how to shorten the summary to 15 words or less without leaving out any essential information. Write this summary below.

_____

_____

_____

2. Choose the best one-sentence paraphrase for the following sentence from the article: "Most of the time, fainting does not signify serious health problems."

☐ a. When you faint, it is usually a sign that you may have a serious health problem.

☐ b. Not everyone who faints should worry about his or her health.

☐ c. Quite often, health problems can cause fainting.

_____ Number of correct answers

Record your personal assessment of your work on the Critical Thinking Chart on page 104.

Critical Thinking

Put an X in the box next to the correct answer for questions 1, 4, and 5. Follow the directions provided for the other questions.

1. From what Doris Goldman said, you can predict that she will

   ☐ a. soon stop warning people about Long QT.

   ☐ b. continue to teach people about Long QT.

   ☐ c. become a doctor herself and treat people with Long QT.

2. Choose from the letters below to correctly complete the following statement. Write the letters on the lines.

   On the positive side, _____, but on the negative side, _____.

   a. many people have died of Long QT

   b. hearts with Long QT have an unusually long time between beats

   c. more and more doctors now know about Long QT

3. Reread paragraph 15. Then choose from the letters below to correctly complete the following statement. Write the letters on the lines.

   According to paragraph 15, _____ because _____.

   a. taking the wrong medicine may bring on Long QT

   b. as people age, their hearts beat more regularly

   c. Long QT is not a problem for old people

4. Of the following theme categories, which would this story fit into?

   ☐ a. Ignorance is bliss.

   ☐ b. What you don't know can kill you.

   ☐ c. A little knowledge is a dangerous thing.

5. What did you have to do to answer question 2

   ☐ a. find an effect (something that happened)

   ☐ b. find a description (how something looks)

   ☐ c. find a contrast (how things are the different)

_____ Number of correct answers

Record your personal assessment of your work on the Critical Thinking Chart on page 104.

Personal Response

Why do you think Doris Goldman decided to teach others about Long QT?

_____

_____

Self-Assessment

One of the things I did best when reading this article was _____

_____

_____

I believe I did this well because _____

_____

_____

The Healing Power of Maggots

Have you ever opened a garbage pail and found maggots swarming around inside? How did you feel? Were you grossed out? Did these wriggling little bugs make you sick to your stomach? These creatures are pretty disgusting. But hold on. Maggots might not really be so creepy after all. In fact, they could save your life!

2 Maggots are the larvae of flies. Flies start out as eggs. Adult female flies often lay their eggs on food, garbage, rotting

Maggots are an early stage of flies. They look like little worms and they eat constantly. Recently, doctors have rediscovered what many ancient healers knew. Because maggots have such a huge appetite for decayed flesh, they can be good medicine!

plants, or dead animals. These eggs look like tiny grains of rice. In a couple of days, the eggs hatch and out crawl the maggots. These maggots are pale yellow or white. They spend most of their time eating. After a few days, the growing maggots reach the point where they turn into flies.

3 It's the eating habits of maggots that make them so helpful. Doctors discovered this during World War I. Wounded soldiers were often stranded on the battlefield for hours and even days. In some cases, their open wounds remained clear. In other cases, their wounds became filled with hundreds of maggots. Doctors found that the soldiers with clear wounds often died. The wounds became infected, sending poison surging through the body. It was the infection more than the wounds themselves that killed these men.

4 But those soldiers with swarming maggots in their wounds had a better record. Many of them survived! Why? The maggots were little eating machines. They constantly searched the wounds for food. Luckily, these maggots had no desire to eat healthy flesh. They craved only decayed flesh and pus. By eating

up the rotten parts of a person's body, they helped to prevent infection. In this way, they saved many lives. The maggots helped in other ways, as well. They released a chemical that killed the germs they didn't eat. Also, by crawling over the good flesh, they gave it a healthy massage.

5 After the war, doctors began to study maggots. They found some interesting things. First, the use of maggots to heal wounds was not really new. It goes back a long way. The Maya peoples of Mexico used maggots more than a thousand years ago. In the 1500s, a French doctor named Ambroise Paré noticed maggots in wounds. He felt at the time that the maggots might be doing some good. Later, Baron D. J. Larrey, another French doctor, praised the work of maggots. He noted that most soldiers were terrified when they saw maggots in their wounds. The soldiers calmed down only when they saw the good these creatures did.

6 By the 1930s, doctors were using maggots as a standard treatment. Drug companies bred maggots and sold them to hospitals. The maggots all came from blow flies. (Maggots from other flies had to be avoided. They would eat healthy

flesh!) An average wound needed about 500 maggots. These maggots would finish their job in two to five days. Then they would turn into flies and fly away.

7　The use of maggots ended in the 1940s. New wonder drugs took their place. At the time, people were very excited about these drugs. The drugs were neat and clean and easy to use. They were much more appealing to patients. Doctors, too, found them more pleasant to use.

8　It is easy to understand why people would prefer drugs to maggots. But was this good science? The new drugs were very expensive. And as it turned out, they didn't always work that well. By the 1990s, doctors were rethinking their position. Said Dr. Jane Petro, "Maggots are more effective and cheaper than a lot of [costly wonder drugs]." Also, maggots are really good at healing tough bone infections. That's because bones have few blood vessels. Modern

drugs, which travel through the bloodstream, can't reach these infections.

9　And so the lowly maggot has been making a mild comeback. Recently a few doctors have started to use them again. Take the case of Dr. Grady Dugas. One of his patients developed deep sores. The sores got infected. They were especially bad on the patient's feet. Dr. Dugas tried using some wonder drugs to clear the sores. None of the drugs seemed to do any good. He then tried surgery to remove the infected tissue. That didn't work either.

10　Dr. Dugas felt he might have to amputate the patient's feet. Then he remembered his grandmother. She had suffered from sores back in the 1930s. Her doctors had treated the sores with maggots. Dugas recalled that the maggots had healed the sores. So he ordered a supply of blow fly eggs. He placed them in his patient's sores. The eggs hatched, and the maggots went to work. They wiped out the infection, and the sores

healed. The maggots had saved the patient's feet!

11　Still, maggots aren't as popular as they could be. Some doctors remain squeamish about using them. And, remember, maggots turn into flies. Not many people want to walk into a hospital filled with flies. So the healing power of maggots remains a well-kept secret. As Dr. Petro put it, "It just goes back to the disgust factor."

If you have been timed while reading this article, enter your reading time below. Then turn to the Words-per-Minute Table on page 101 and look up your reading speed (words per minute). Enter your reading speed on the graph on page 102.

Reading Time: Lesson 8

—————— : ——————
Minutes　　*Seconds*

A | Finding the Main Idea

One statement below expresses the main idea of the article. One statement is too general, or too broad. The other statement explains only part of the article; it is too narrow. Label the statements using the following key:

M—Main Idea   **B—Too Broad**   **N—Too Narrow**

_____ 1. Modern medicine is rediscovering that maggots can wipe out the infection in an open wound or sore.

_____ 2. The use of maggots to heal wounds is not new.

_____ 3. Some ancient methods of curing illnesses have been shown to be as effective as modern drugs.

_____ Score 15 points for a correct M answer.

_____ Score 5 points for each correct B or N answer.

_____ **Total Score:** Finding the Main Idea

B | Recalling Facts

How well do you remember the facts in the article? Put an X in the box next to the answer that correctly completes each statement about the article.

1. A few days after female flies lay eggs,
   □ a. maggots crawl out of the eggs.
   □ b. baby flies hatch and fly away.
   □ c. the eggs turn pale yellow or white.

2. American doctors recognized the benefits of maggots in healing wounds during
   □ a. the Civil War.
   □ b. World War I.
   □ c. the Korean War.

3. Maggots help to cure wounds by
   □ a. eating the rotten parts of a person's body.
   □ b. keeping patient's thoughts on the maggots.
   □ c. eating healthy flesh.

4. The earliest known use of maggots to heal was
   □ a. more than a thousand years ago.
   □ b. in the 1500s.
   □ c. in the 1700s.

5. Reasons for using maggots today do *not* include
   □ a. the higher cost of new drugs.
   □ b. the fact that maggots are more effective than drugs on bone infections.
   □ c. the squeamish attitude of patients and doctors.

Score 5 points for each correct answer.

_____ **Total Score:** Recalling Facts

C | Making Inferences

When you combine your own experience with information from a text to draw a conclusion that is not directly stated in that text, you are making an inference. Below are five statements that may or may not be inferences based on information in the article. Label the statements using the following key:

C—Correct Inference   F—Faulty Inference

_____ 1. Researchers probably took samples of patients' skin to determine how maggots had helped them.

_____ 2. There may be other examples of "folk medicine" that modern medicine does not yet make use of.

_____ 3. The average person could care for his or her own wounds by applying fly eggs to them.

_____ 4. It might be difficult for a doctor to get the approval of both the patient and the hospital for treatment with maggots.

_____ 5. It is likely that we will hear more about treatment with maggots in the near future.

Score 5 points for each correct answer.

_____ **Total Score:** Making Inferences

D | Using Words Precisely

Each numbered sentence below contains an underlined word or phrase from the article. Following the sentence are three definitions. One definition is closest to the meaning of the underlined word. One definition is opposite or nearly opposite. Label those two definitions using the following key; do not label the remaining definition.

C—Closest   O—Opposite or Nearly Opposite

1. Wounded soldiers were often <u>stranded</u> on the battlefield for hours and even days.

_____ a. rescued

_____ b. imprisoned

_____ c. left

2. They <u>craved</u> only decayed flesh and pus.

_____ a. desired

_____ b. rejected

_____ c. observed

3. They <u>released</u> a chemical that killed the germs they didn't eat.

_____ a. described

_____ b. sent out

_____ c. held back

4. Dr. Dugas felt that he might have to <u>amputate</u> the patient's feet.

_____ a. give up on

_____ b. reattach

_____ c. cut off

5. Some doctors remain <u>squeamish</u> about them.

_____ ☐ a. easily upset

_____ ☐ b. likely to giggle

_____ ☐ c. undisturbed

_____ Score 3 points for each correct C answer.

_____ Score 2 points for each correct O answer.

_____ **Total Score:** Using Words Precisely

Enter the four total scores in the spaces below, and add them together to find your Reading Comprehension Score. Then record your score on the graph on page 103.

Score	Question Type	Lesson 8
_____	Finding the Main Idea	
_____	Recalling Facts	
_____	Making Inferences	
_____	Using Words Precisely	
_____	**Reading Comprehension Score**	

Author's Approach

Put an X in the box next to the correct answer.

1. The main purpose of the first paragraph is to

☐ a. explain how maggots can be useful.

☐ b. define what maggots are.

☐ c. help readers become personally involved in the subject of maggots.

2. From the statements below, choose those that you believe the authors would agree with.

☐ a. Most people find maggots disgusting.

☐ b. Maggots help wounds by eating decayed flesh and pus.

☐ c. Maggots have only recently been used to heal wounds.

3. Choose the statement below that is the weakest argument for using maggots to treat wounds.

☐ a. Maggots release a chemical that kills germs.

☐ b. Maggots eat the rotten parts of a wound.

☐ c. Using maggots to treat wounds began long ago.

4. In this article, "And so the lowly maggot has been making a mild comeback" means

☐ a. all doctors now want to use maggots to treat their patients.

☐ b. a few doctors are willing to try using maggots when other treatments have failed.

☐ c. doctors and patients no longer feel the maggot is disgusting.

_____ Number of correct answers

Record your personal assessment of your work on the Critical Thinking Chart on page 104.

Summarizing and Paraphrasing

Follow the directions provided for question 1. Put an X in the box next to the correct answer for the other questions.

1. Look for the important ideas and events in paragraphs 9 and 10. Summarize those paragraphs in one or two sentences.

_____

_____

_____

2. Below are summaries of the article. Choose the summary that says all the most important things about the article but in the fewest words.

☐ a. Most patients are not pleased when they look down to see maggots crawling on their wounds. However, maggots do give many patients a new chance to improve. They eat up the rotten parts of a wound.

☐ b. Maggots are the larvae of flies. They live as maggots for only a few days. During those days, they spend most of their time eating. Then they turn into flies. Doctors are finding many uses for maggots.

☐ c. Maggots, the larvae of flies, have been used for many years to treat wounds. They attack decayed flesh and pus and help the wounds heal. After being used by doctors during the 1930s and 1940s, they disappeared from the medical scene. Now they are becoming popular again with some doctors.

3. Choose the best one-sentence paraphrase for the following sentence from the article: "Not many people want to walk into a hospital filled with flies."

☐ a. People with flies hardly ever want to walk into the hospital.

☐ b. Hospitals are not good places for people with flies.

☐ c. Most people don't want to see flies in their hospitals.

_____ Number of correct answers

Record your personal assessment of your work on the Critical Thinking Chart on page 104.

Critical Thinking

Put an X in the box next to the correct answer for questions 1, 4, and 5. Follow the directions provided for the other questions.

1. Which of the following statements from the article is an opinion rather than a fact?

☐ a. These creatures are pretty disgusting.

☐ b. After the war, doctors began to study maggots.

☐ c. The Maya peoples of Mexico used maggots more than a thousand years ago.

2. Choose from the letters below to correctly complete the following statement. Write the letters on the lines.

On the positive side, _____, but on the negative side, _____.

a. maggots are the larvae of flies

b. maggots sometimes aid healing

c. maggots frighten some patients

CRITICAL THINKING

3. Think about cause-effect relationships in the article. Fill in the blanks in the cause-effect chart, drawing from the letters below.

Cause	Effect
Maggots look creepy.	_____
Some maggots eat healthy flesh.	_____
_____	Some doctors are trying maggot treatment instead of drug treatment.

a. Doctors are careful about which kind of maggot they use on wounds.

b. Doctors have found that wonder drugs don't always work.

c. Most patients don't like maggot treatment at first.

4. Of the following theme categories, which would this story fit into?

☐ a. Just because a treatment can be described as natural doesn't mean it is good.

☐ b. Doing a job well is more important than looking good while you do it.

☐ c. Trust your feelings. If something seems disgusting, stay away from it.

5. What did you have to do to answer question 1?

☐ a. find an opinion (what someone thinks about something)

☐ b. find a definition (what something means)

☐ c. find an effect (something that happened)

_____ Number of correct answers

Record your personal assessment of your work on the Critical Thinking Chart on page 104.

Personal Response

How do you think you would feel if a doctor suggested a maggot treatment for a wound on your arm or leg?

_____

_____

_____

Self-Assessment

I was confused on question _____ in the _____ section

because _____

_____

_____

Psychics Who Solve Crimes

On December 3, 1967, Dorothy Allison had a frightening dream. In it, she saw the body of a small boy in a river. Allison tried to forget about the dream. But she couldn't. At last she called the police in her town of Nutley, New Jersey. It turned out that a five-year-old boy had indeed drowned in a local river. But he had fallen into the water two hours after Dorothy Allison's dream.

Some people claim that they can "see" events that happen far away from them. These people, called psychics, can't explain how they obtain their information. But what they know may give clues to police stumped by mysterious crimes.

2   When Allison called the police, they were still looking for the boy's body. They did not want to be bothered by housewives with wild dreams. The tragedy had been reported in the newspapers. So police figured Allison had learned about it there. But Dorothy Allison knew things that had not been printed in the papers. For instance, she said she could see what the boy was wearing.

3   Police Officer Donald Vicaro was intrigued. He asked Allison what else she could "see." Allison told him that the boy's shoes were on the wrong feet. She said she saw a number "8" and a school with a fence around it. She also saw a gray house and a factory.

4   A few weeks later, the boy's body was finally found. It had been washed downstream into a nearby pond. When Officer Vicaro arrived at the scene, he could hardly believe his eyes. There, next to the pond, was Public School Number 8. Around the school was a fence. A factory stood in the distance and so did a gray house. Vicaro checked the boy's body. As Dorothy Allison had predicted, the shoes were on the wrong feet!

5   Dorothy Allison is a psychic. She seems to have special powers to "see" things. Some of her visions come from faraway places. Some come from the future; others come from the past. Allison is not sure how or why she has these visions. She only knows that she's been getting them since childhood.

6   After the case of the boy who had drowned, police asked Allison to help solve other crimes. By 1987, she had helped crack hundreds of cases. She does not take any pay for her work. She is just happy when her visions can be put to good use. Often Allison herself does not know what her visions mean. As one detective says, "she may see things backwards, forwards, in the middle. . . . It's up to the police to put the information in some kind of order." Adds one sheriff, "Working with a psychic is like doing a crossword puzzle!"

7   Allison is not the only psychic who has helped solve crimes. There are hundreds like her. In Delavan, Illinois, police sometimes turn to Greta Alexander. In 1977 Alexander told police where to find two drowned

victims. Six years later, she helped out again. A woman had been missing for a month. Alexander told police to go to a wooded spot near the town of Peoria. There, she said, the woman's body would be found near a bridge. A pile of rocks or salt would also be found there. She warned police that the woman's head would be detached from her body. Alexander was right on all counts.

8   Pennsylvania psychic Nancy Czetli has worked on more than a hundred cases. She has helped solve murders. She has helped find kidnappers and track down burglars. In January of 1988, she was asked to find a 78-year-old man who had gone out for a walk but never returned. Police had searched for him for a week. They had used dogs, a helicopter—everything. They had found no trace of him. Yet when Czetli looked at an old photograph of the man, she could sense right away what had happened. He had died from the cold. Czetli pointed out the path he had followed. She led police right to the spot where his body was found.

9   Texas psychic John Catchings began working with police in 1980. He was

asked to help find an 18-year-old boy who had disappeared. Catchings felt at once that the boy had been murdered. He asked to hold something that had belonged to the boy. He was given the boy's high school ring. "When I held the ring," Catchings says, "I saw a white house with peeling paint, a trail behind the house, weeds, an old tire, a shoe, a creek."

10   Police recognized the place Catchings described. It was near the missing boy's home. Catchings announced that the boy's body would be found there. "An old shoe will be the marker," he said. "You'll find the boy's left heel and ankle exposed."

11   Police had already searched the property once. But they decided to look again. Sure enough, this time they noticed a tree with tires piled up around it. On top of one tire was a sandal. Could that be the shoe Catchings mentioned? When police moved the tires, they saw a heel sticking out of the ground. Digging

up the dirt, they found the body of the missing boy.

12   Psychics work in a variety of ways. Some "see" crimes in their dreams. Some say they can read the mind of a victim. Even after a person has died, they say, his or her thought patterns linger on in the brain. By reading those patterns, they can find out what happened. "I don't become the victim," says Nancy Czetli, "but it's as if I'm standing alongside him."

13   Many psychics also use psychometry. This involves getting information from objects. Psychics may ask to hold something that belonged to the victim. It could be anything. It could be an old hat or— as in John Catchings's famous case—a high school ring. Psychics say they can get vibrations from these things. By feeling the vibrations, they can tell what happened to the object's owner.

14   Psychics have not convinced everyone. Some people still scoff at them. Dr. Martin Reiser has done studies for the Los Angeles Police

Department. He says psychics are of no use to police. But more and more people are echoing the words of Detective Ron Phillips. "I felt it was baloney at first," he said. But then Phillips worked with John Catchings. "He made me believe [in psychics]," Phillips said. "They've got a power there—it gives you goose bumps, really."

If you have been timed while reading this article, enter your reading time below. Then turn to the Words-per-Minute Table on page 101 and look up your reading speed (words per minute). Enter your reading speed on the graph on page 102.

Reading Time: Lesson 9

——————— : ———————
Minutes   Seconds

A Finding the Main Idea

One statement below expresses the main idea of the article. One statement is too general, or too broad. The other statement explains only part of the article; it is too narrow. Label the statements using the following key:

M—Main Idea   **B—Too Broad**   **N—Too Narrow**

_____ 1. Psychics have a special knowledge of things that have happened or are about to happen.

_____ 2. Psychics' ability to "see" things that others can't makes them valuable in solving crimes.

_____ 3. Psychic Nancy Czetli has been helpful in solving cases of murder, kidnapping, and burglary.

_____ Score 15 points for a correct M answer.

_____ Score 5 points for each correct B or N answer.

_____ **Total Score:** Finding the Main Idea

B Recalling Facts

How well do you remember the facts in the article? Put an X in the box next to the answer that correctly completes each statement about the article.

1. At first, police ignored Dorothy Allison's offer to help because they
   - ☐ a. thought she read about it in the newspaper.
   - ☐ b. had all the clues they needed.
   - ☐ c. didn't like housewives.

2. One amazing detail Allison had "seen" was that the
   - ☐ a. boy was carrying $100.
   - ☐ b. boy's hair was red.
   - ☐ c. boy's shoes were on the wrong feet.

3. More police are asking for help from psychics because
   - ☐ a. psychics usually work for free.
   - ☐ b. they want one more way to fight crime.
   - ☐ c. regular ways of solving crimes never work.

4. John Catchings was handed a missing boy's
   - ☐ a. high school ring.
   - ☐ b. team jacket.
   - ☐ c. wallet.

5. Some psychics say that when they hold an object that belongs to a victim, they
   - ☐ a. can hear the voice of the victim.
   - ☐ b. become the victim themselves.
   - ☐ c. get vibrations from the object.

Score 5 points for each correct answer.

_____ **Total Score:** Recalling Facts

C Making Inferences

When you combine your own experience with information from a text to draw a conclusion that is not directly stated in that text, you are making an inference. Below are five statements that may or may not be inferences based on information in the article. Label the statements using the following key:

C—Correct Inference   **F—Faulty Inference**

_____ 1. Psychic Dorothy Allison is usually thought to be a greedy person.

_____ 2. Psychics may be born with their unusual powers.

_____ 3. Psychics do their best work in their hometowns.

_____ 4. Police departments usually bring psychics in on their cases after usual methods have failed.

_____ 5. It takes clever police work to use the information that psychics give.

Score 5 points for each correct answer.

_____ **Total Score:** Making Inferences

D Using Words Precisely

Each numbered sentence below contains an underlined word or phrase from the article. Following the sentence are three definitions. One definition is closest to the meaning of the underlined word. One definition is opposite or nearly opposite. Label those two definitions using the following key; do not label the remaining definition.

C—Closest   **O—Opposite or Nearly Opposite**

1. The <u>tragedy</u> had been reported in the newspapers.

_____ a. story

_____ b. comedy

_____ c. sad event

2. Police Officer Donald Vicaro was <u>intrigued</u>.

_____ a. greatly interested

_____ b. stubborn

_____ c. uncaring

3. She warned police that the woman's head would be <u>detached</u> from her body.

_____ a. attached

_____ b. separated

_____ c. different

4. You'll find the boy's left heel and ankle <u>exposed</u>.

_____ a. hidden

_____ b. dirty

_____ c. uncovered

5. Even after a person has died, they say, his or her thought patterns <u>linger</u> on in the brain.

_____ a. read

_____ b. stay

_____ c. leave

_____ Score 3 points for each correct C answer.

_____ Score 2 points for each correct O answer.

_____ **Total Score:** Using Words Precisely

Enter the four total scores in the spaces below, and add them together to find your Reading Comprehension Score. Then record your score on the graph on page 103.

Score	Question Type	Lesson 9
_____	Finding the Main Idea	
_____	Recalling Facts	
_____	Making Inferences	
_____	Using Words Precisely	
_____	**Reading Comprehension Score**	

Author's Approach

Put an X in the box next to the correct answer.

1. The main purpose of the first paragraph is to

☐ a. emphasize the special powers of one particular psychic.

☐ b. tell readers about a famous crime.

☐ c. show how frightening dreams can be.

2. Which of the following statements from the article best describes one method that psychics use, called psychometry?

☐ a. Some [psychics] say they can read the mind of a victim.

☐ b. Some [psychics] "see" crimes in their dreams.

☐ c. Psychics may ask to hold something that belonged to the victim.

3. In this article, "Working with a psychic is like doing a crossword puzzle" means

☐ a. Psychics think that solving crimes is a game, so they purposely keep important information to themselves. Whoever works with them will get frustrated.

☐ b. Psychics don't fill in all the missing pieces. Whoever works with a psychic has to pick up on clues that the psychic supplies.

☐ c. To solve a case when working with a psychic is almost impossible.

_____ Number of correct answers

Record your personal assessment of your work on the Critical Thinking Chart on page 104.

Summarizing and Paraphrasing

Follow the directions provided for question 1. Put an X in the box next to the correct answer for question 2.

1. Reread paragraph 8 in the article. Below, write a summary of the paragraph in no more than 25 words.

_____

_____

_____

Reread your summary and decide whether it covers the important ideas in the paragraph. Next, decide how to shorten the summary to 15 words or less without leaving out any essential information. Write this summary below.

_____

_____

_____

2. Read the statement from the article below. Then read the paraphrase of that statement. Choose the reason that best tells why the paraphrase does not say the same thing as the statement.

   Statement: When John Catchings described the place where the body was, police recognized it immediately.

   Paraphrase: Police were puzzled when John Catchings described the place where he thought the body would be found.

☐ a. Paraphrase says too much.

☐ b. Paraphrase doesn't say enough.

☐ c. Paraphrase doesn't agree with the statement.

_____ Number of correct answers

Record your personal assessment of your work on the Critical Thinking Chart on page 104.

Critical Thinking

Follow the directions provided for questions 1, 3, and 5. Put an X in the box next to the correct answer for the other questions.

1. For each statement below, write *O* if it expresses an opinion or write *F* if it expresses a fact.

   _____ a. Not everyone believes in the power of psychics.

   _____ b. Working with psychics is spooky.

   _____ c. People who say they are psychics are just fooling.

2. From what Detective Ron Phillips said, you can predict that he will

☐ a. stay away from psychics because they scare him.

☐ b. be willing to ask a psychic for help.

☐ c. always go to psychics first before he tries regular methods of solving any case.

3. Choose from the letters below to correctly complete the following statement. Write the letters on the lines.

   In the article, _____ and _____ are alike in their opinions about psychics.

   a. Dr. Martin Reiser

   b. Detective Ron Phillips

   c. Police Officer Donald Vicaro

4. What was the cause of the 78-year-old man's death, according to psychic Nancy Czetli?

   ☐ a. He died from the cold.

   ☐ b. He had been murdered.

   ☐ c. He had drowned.

5. Which paragraphs from the article provide evidence that supports your answer to question 3?_____

_____ Number of correct answers

Record your personal assessment of your work on the Critical Thinking Chart on page 104.

Personal Response

I know the feeling that Dorothy Allison had after her dream because _____

_____

_____

_____

Self-Assessment

I can't really understand how _____

_____

_____

_____

_____

Mummies

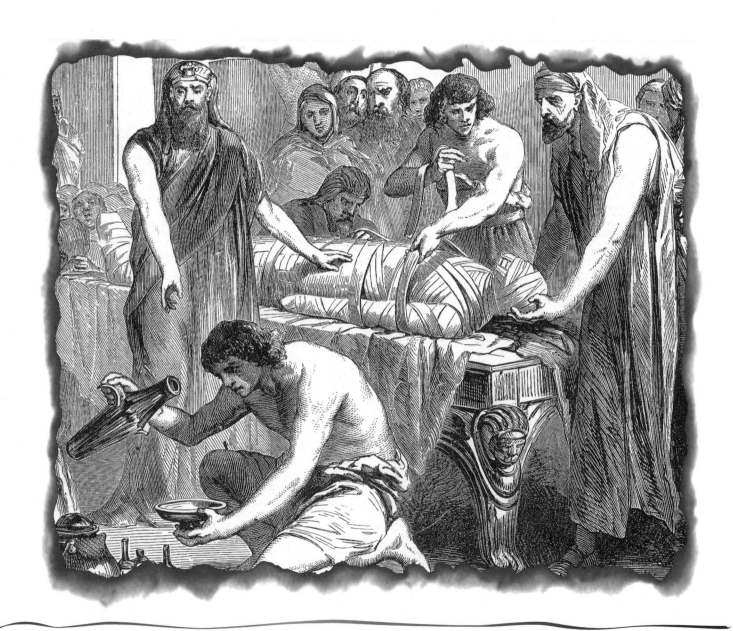

Have you ever thought of being a mummy for Halloween? You could probably do it just by wrapping yourself in a bunch of white bandages.

But making a real mummy is not so easy. First, you need a dead body. And second, you need someone who understands the ancient art of mummy making.

2   A mummy is not the same as a skeleton. A skeleton is just bones. But a mummy has bones and skin. Often

The people of ancient Egypt believed that spirits of the dead still needed their bodies in the afterlife. So after people died, their bodies were given special treatment to keep them from decaying. Bodies undergoing this complicated treatment are called mummies.

it has hair, fingernails, and muscles as well. Usually, these softer body parts decay quickly. But that does not happen with mummies. If a mummy has been properly prepared, it can last a long, long time.

3   Ancient Egyptians were master mummy makers. Some of their mummies are now more than three thousand years old. These bodies still have lips, noses, and ears. They have eyelids and toenails. One has red hair. Another has a face twisted in a scream of death made thousands of years ago.

4   How did the Egyptians make such great mummies? Their secret was to dry each body thoroughly. If a body is totally dry, the flesh won't rot away. Drying a body means getting rid of all the fluids in it. To do this, Egyptians slit open the side of each body. They scooped out much of the insides. They took out the stomach. They took out the liver, intestines, and lungs. They did not take out the heart, however. They believed the heart was the center of wisdom and truth. So they left that alone.

5   The brain was removed thrugh the nose. Mummy makers stuck a long metal hook up the nose of the body.

They scrambled the brain and partially liquefied it. Then they stored it and other organs in jars.

6   Once Egyptians had cleaned out a body, they washed it with wine. They packed it with a special salt called natron. Then they sat back and waited for 40 days. During that time, the natron soaked up liquid from the body. By the end of the 40 days, no liquid was left.

7   The drying-out process left bodies as shriveled as prunes. But Egyptians solved that problem too. They stuffed the bodies with cloth or sand. That puffed the skin back up again. Sometimes they put peppercorns up the nose. That helped push the nose back to its original shape. Egyptians also rubbed spices and herbs on the body to mask the smell of death.

8   Next, mummy makers coated the dried body with a glue called resin. As the resin dried, it became hard. It formed a tough coating that protected the body. It made the body waterproof.

9   Finally, Egyptians wrapped each body in 20 layers of cloth. This was a tricky task. It took many days and required about 150 yards of cloth. Sometimes

an ear or toe fell off during the wrapping. But by the time the last layer was put on, the mummy was close to normal size again.

10 From 2600 B.C. to A.D. 300, Egyptians made millions of mummies. Almost everyone in Egypt who could afford it became one. Egyptians also mummified animals. They made cat mummies and dog mummies. They turned fish, snakes, and birds into mummies. They even made mummies out of grasshoppers and beetles!

11 There was a reason for this "mummy mania." Egyptians thought living things needed their bodies after death. They believed dead people went on to the land of the gods. Even dead animals moved on to an "afterlife." Spirits of the dead could make contact with the gods. But those spirits still needed a place to rest at night. They needed to return to their bodies. If their bodies had rotted away, the spirits would have no place to rest. Then the spirits, too, would die.

12 Ancient Egyptians were not the only ones who believed in life after death. And they were not the only ones who made mummies. Halfway across the world, in the mountains of South America, people did the same thing. By 3000 B.C., people in Peru and Chile had figured out how to preserve dead bodies. They did not dry them with salt. Instead, they set them out in the hot sun. Sometimes they also put them over a fire. The heat and smoke helped to get rid of all liquids. Once the bodies were dry, they were wrapped up and put in baskets. In Egypt, mummies were stretched out flat. But most South American mummies had their knees folded up to their chins.

13 Mummies are not always thousands of years old. About 400 years ago, some people in Italy started making mummies. They felt it would help them keep in touch with the spirits of those who had died. These Italians put the bodies in a special room. They left them there for a year. During that time, all fluids drained out of the bodies. Then the bodies were laid in the sun. When they were fully dried, they were dressed in fancy clothes. They were put in underground rooms called catacombs.

14 People often visited the mummies in the catacombs. They brought picnic lunches to eat. They talked to the mummies, asking them for advice. Some people even held hands with the mummies as they said prayers.

15 The last Italian mummy was created in 1920. It was made from the body of a little girl named Rosali Lombardo. Rosali died at the age of two. Her father was a doctor. He knew how to mummify dead bodies. In fact, he had developed a new system for it. Dr. Lombardo used his system on little Rosali. The results were amazing. Rosali's body is perfectly preserved. It has not shriveled at all. In fact, it looks as though Rosali is just taking a nap. No one knows what Dr. Lombardo's system was. He died before sharing it with the world.

16 Some people think mummies are a good way to honor the dead. But others don't even like to look at them. You might want to keep that in mind if you ever do dress up like a mummy for Halloween.

If you have been timed while reading this article, enter your reading time below. Then turn to the Words-per-Minute Table on page 101 and look up your reading speed (words per minute). Enter your reading speed on the graph on page 102.

Reading Time: Lesson 10

_____ : _____
Minutes   *Seconds*

A Finding the Main Idea

One statement below expresses the main idea of the article. One statement is too general, or too broad. The other statement explains only part of the article; it is too narrow. Label the statements using the following key:

M—Main Idea   **B—Too Broad**   **N—Too Narrow**

_____ 1. Many people around the world and in different times shared a belief in an afterlife, and this belief affected burial customs.

_____ 2. Although other people have made mummies, too, the process used by ancient Egyptians is the best known.

_____ 3. Many mummies have not only bones and skin, but also hair, fingernails, and muscles.

_____ Score 15 points for a correct M answer.

_____ Score 5 points for each correct B or N answer.

_____ **Total Score:** Finding the Main Idea

B Recalling Facts

How well do you remember the facts in the article? Put an X in the box next to the answer that correctly completes each statement about the article.

1. The first step in making a mummy is to
☐ a. dry the body thoroughly.
☐ b. remove most inner organs and the brain.
☐ c. wrap the body in layers of cloth.

2. The Egyptians used a glue called resin to
☐ a. give the dried-out body a natural shape.
☐ b. glue onto the body any small parts, such as ears and toes, that had fallen off.
☐ c. waterproof the body.

3. The Egyptians thought that, at death, a spirit
☐ a. died along with its body.
☐ b. left the body forever to go to the gods.
☐ c. visited the gods but returned to its body to rest.

4. Mummies made in South America usually
☐ a. were dressed in fancy clothes.
☐ b. had their knees folded up to their chins.
☐ c. were buried in large wooden boxes.

5. Italians who made mummies during the last 400 years did so in order to
☐ a. keep in touch with the spirits of the dead.
☐ b. display the mummies in museums.
☐ c. save the bodies of the dead for future cures.

Score 5 points for each correct answer.

_____ **Total Score:** Recalling Facts

C | Making Inferences

When you combine your own experience with information from a text to draw a conclusion that is not directly stated in that text, you are making an inference. Below are five statements that may or may not be inferences based on information in the article. Label the statements using the following key:

C—Correct Inference　　　**F—Faulty Inference**

_____ 1. In ancient Egypt, the process of making a human body into a mummy cost a great deal.

_____ 2. Making mummies is easier in desert areas than in rainy lands.

_____ 3. The people of South America got the idea of making mummies from the people of Egypt.

_____ 4. Ancient Egyptians would think that a Halloween mummy costume shows disrespect for the dead.

_____ 5. Doctors in ancient Egypt had a good idea of how each part of the body worked and what it did for the living person.

Score 5 points for each correct answer.

_____ **Total Score:** Making Inferences

D | Using Words Precisely

Each numbered sentence below contains an underlined word or phrase from the article. Following the sentence are three definitions. One definition is closest to the meaning of the underlined word. One definition is opposite or nearly opposite. Label those two definitions using the following key; do not label the remaining definition.

C—Closest　　　**O—Opposite or Nearly Opposite**

1. Usually, these softer body parts <u>decay</u> quickly.

_____ a. grow

_____ b. shake

_____ c. rot

2. Their secret was to dry each body <u>thoroughly</u>.

_____ a. completely

_____ b. at a high altitude

_____ c. imperfectly

3. The drying-out process left bodies as <u>shriveled</u> as prunes.

_____ a. colorful

_____ b. shrunken and wrinkled

_____ c. swollen

4. Even dead animals moved on to an "<u>afterlife</u>."

_____ a. nothingness

_____ b. life after death

_____ c. judgment

5. By 3000 B.C., people in Peru and Chile had figured out how to <u>preserve</u> dead bodies.

_____ a. keep

_____ b. display

_____ c. destroy

_____ Score 3 points for each correct C answer.

_____ Score 2 points for each correct O answer.

_____ **Total Score:** Using Words Precisely

Enter the four total scores in the spaces below, and add them together to find your Reading Comprehension Score. Then record your score on the graph on page 103.

Score	Question Type	Lesson 10
_____	Finding the Main Idea	
_____	Recalling Facts	
_____	Making Inferences	
_____	Using Words Precisely	
_____	**Reading Comprehension Score**	

Author's Approach

Put an X in the box next to the correct answer.

1. What do the authors imply by saying "Egyptians also mummified animals"?

☐ a. Egyptians thought animals had spirits that lived on after death.

☐ b. Egyptians thought that animal mummies were nice decorations for the tombs of their loved ones.

☐ c. Egyptians who made mummies worked on animals when they had nothing else to do.

2. The authors probably wrote this article to

☐ a. inform the reader about a fascinating custom that requires scientific know-how.

☐ b. show admiration for people who know how to mummify dead bodies.

☐ c. point out the difference between the beliefs of people in ancient times and the beliefs of people today.

3. The authors tell this story mainly by

☐ a. retelling personal experiences.

☐ b. using his or her imagination and creativity.

☐ c. telling different accounts of the same topic.

_____ Number of correct answers

Record your personal assessment of your work on the Critical Thinking Chart on page 104.

Summarizing and Paraphrasing

Follow the directions provided for question 1. Put an X in the box next to the correct answer for other questions.

1. Complete the following one-sentence summary of the article using the lettered phrases from the phrase bank below. Write the letters on the lines.

> **Phrase Bank:**
> a. mummies in Italy
> b. mummies in South America
> c. mummies in ancient Egypt

The article "Mummies" begins with _____, goes on to explain _____, and ends with _____.

2. Below are summaries of the article. Choose the summary that says all the most important things about the article but in the fewest words.

☐ a. Ancient Egyptians are famous for their skill in making mummies. In their process, most of the body's internal organs were taken out and the body was dried out completely. After stuffing the shriveled body with cloth or sand, Egyptians applied a glue to the body and then wrapped it in layers of cloth.

☐ b. For thousands of years, people around the world have preserved dead bodies as mummies. To make a mummy, the body must first be drained of liquid and then dried out completely. Different cultures completed the process in different ways.

☐ c. Mummies in Egypt were laid out flat in their coffins, but most mummies of South America were arranged with their knees folded up to their chins. Italian mummies were dressed in fancy clothes and laid to rest in catacombs.

3. Choose the sentence that correctly restates the following sentence from the article: "Once Egyptians had cleaned out a body, they washed it with wine."

☐ a. Egyptians washed the body with wine after it had been cleaned out.

☐ b. After washing it with wine, the Egyptians cleaned out the body.

☐ c. Egyptians cleaned the body with wine and then washed it thoroughly.

> _____ Number of correct answers
>
> Record your personal assessment of your work on the Critical Thinking Chart on page 104.

Critical Thinking

Put an X in the box next to the correct answer questions 1 and 4. Follow the directions provided for the other questions.

1. Which of the following statements from the article is an opinion rather than a fact?

☐ a. From 2600 B.C. to A.D. 300, Egyptians made millions of mummies.

☐ b. The last Italian mummy was created in 1920.

☐ c. The results were amazing.

2. Choose from the letters below to correctly complete the following statement. Write the letters on the lines.

In the article, _____ and _____ are different.

a. the way Egyptians treated the brain of the mummy

b. the way Egyptians treated the heart of the mummy

c. the way Egyptians treated the lungs of the mummy

3. Choose from the letters below to correctly complete the following statement. Write the letters on the lines.

According to the article, Egyptians believed that if the dead body rotted, the spirits of the dead _____, and the effect was that the spirits _____.

a. died

b. were mummies

c. had no place to rest

4. If you were a taxidermist (someone who stuffs and mounts dead animals), how could you use the information in the article to do your job?

☐ a. Like the Italians, you would dress the body in fancy clothes.

☐ b. Your first step would be to dry the body out completely.

☐ c. You would need to believe that the spirit of the dead animal needed its body in order to rest at night.

5. In which paragraph did you find your information or details to answer question 3? _____

_____ Number of correct answers

Record your personal assessment of your work on the Critical Thinking Chart on page 104.

Personal Response

What new question do you have about this topic?

_____

_____

_____

_____

Self-Assessment

Before reading this article, I already knew _____

_____

_____

_____

Compare and Contrast

Think about the articles you have read in Unit Two. Pick the three articles that were most complicated or confusing. Write the titles of those articles in the first column of the chart below. Use information you learned from the articles to fill in the empty boxes in the chart.

Title	What idea or process does the article discuss?	Which parts of the article were confusing to you?	Which parts of the article made the most sense?

If I could speak to the authors, I would ask them to explain this part of the article to me: _____

_____

_____

Words-per-Minute Table

Unit Two

Directions: If you were timed while reading an article, refer to the Reading Time you recorded in the box at the end of the article. Use this Words-per-Minute Table to determine your reading speed for that article. Then plot your reading speed on the graph on page 102.

Lesson No. of Words	6 1,058	7 1,139	8 850	9 1,043	10 1,014	Seconds
1:30	705	759	567	695	676	**90**
1:40	635	683	510	626	608	**100**
1:50	577	621	464	569	553	**110**
2:00	529	570	425	522	507	**120**
2:10	488	526	392	481	468	**130**
2:20	453	488	364	447	435	**140**
2:30	423	456	340	417	406	**150**
2:40	397	427	319	391	380	**160**
2:50	373	402	300	368	358	**170**
3:00	353	380	283	348	338	**180**
3:10	334	360	268	329	320	**190**
3:20	317	342	255	313	304	**200**
3:30	302	325	243	298	390	**210**
3:40	289	311	232	284	277	**220**
3:50	276	297	222	272	265	**230**
4:00	265	285	213	261	254	**240**
4:10	254	273	204	250	243	**250**
4:20	244	263	196	241	234	**260**
4:30	235	253	189	232	225	**270**
4:40	227	244	182	224	217	**280**
4:50	219	236	176	216	210	**290**
5:00	212	228	170	209	203	**300**
5:10	205	220	165	202	196	**310**
5:20	198	214	159	196	190	**320**
5:30	192	207	155	190	184	**330**
5:40	187	201	150	184	179	**340**
5:50	181	195	146	179	174	**350**
6:00	176	190	142	174	169	**360**
6:10	172	185	138	169	164	**370**
6:20	167	180	134	165	160	**380**
6:30	163	175	131	160	156	**390**
6:40	159	171	128	156	152	**400**
6:50	155	167	124	153	148	**410**
7:00	151	163	121	149	145	**420**
7:10	148	159	119	146	141	**430**
7:20	144	155	116	142	138	**440**
7:30	141	152	113	139	135	**450**
7:40	138	149	111	136	132	**460**
7:50	135	145	109	133	129	**470**
8:00	132	142	106	130	127	**480**

Minutes and Seconds

Plotting Your Progress: Reading Speed

Unit Two

Directions: If you were timed while reading an article, write your words-per-minute rate for that article in the box under the number of the lesson. Then plot your reading speed on the graph by putting a small X on the line directly above the number of the lesson, across from the number of words per minute you read. As you mark your speed for each lesson, graph your progress by drawing a line to connect the X's.

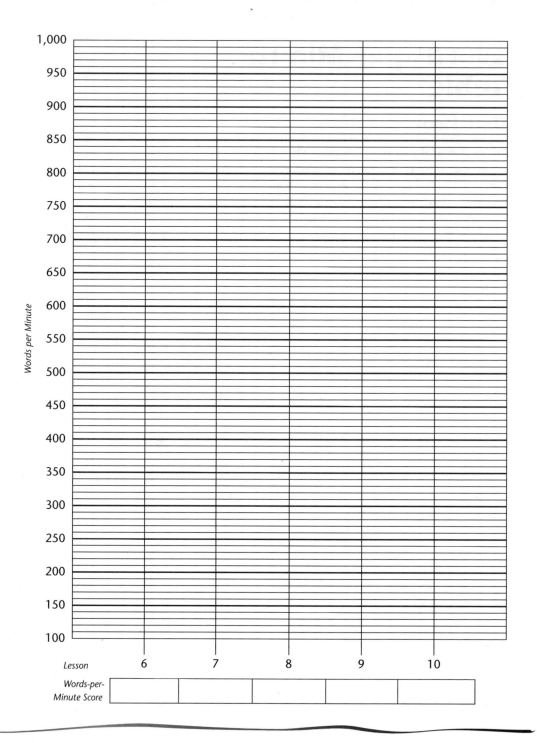

Words per Minute

| 1,000 |
| 950 |
| 900 |
| 850 |
| 800 |
| 750 |
| 700 |
| 650 |
| 600 |
| 550 |
| 500 |
| 450 |
| 400 |
| 350 |
| 300 |
| 250 |
| 200 |
| 150 |
| 100 |

Lesson	6	7	8	9	10
Words-per-Minute Score					

Plotting Your Progress: Reading Comprehension

Unit Two

Directions: Write your Reading Comprehension Score for each lesson in the box under the number of the lesson. Then plot your score on the graph by putting a small X on the line directly above the number of the lesson and across from the score you earned. As you mark your score for each lesson, graph your progress by drawing a line to connect the X's.

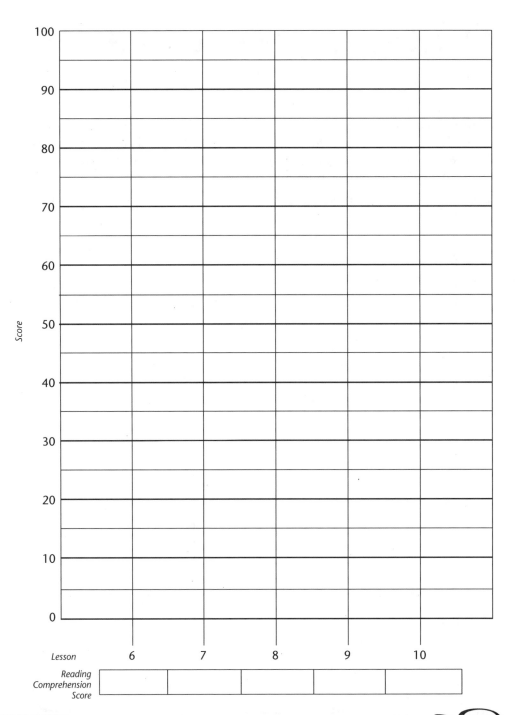

Lesson	6	7	8	9	10
Reading Comprehension Score					

Plotting Your Progress: Critical Thinking

Unit Two

Directions: Work with your teacher to evaluate your responses to the Critical Thinking questions for each lesson. Then fill in the appropriate spaces in the chart below. For each lesson and each type of Critical Thinking question, do the following: Mark a minus sign (–) in the box to indicate areas in which you feel you could improve. Mark a plus sign (+) to indicate areas in which you feel you did well. Mark a minus-slash-plus sign (–/+) to indicate areas in which you had mixed success. Then write any comments you have about your performance, including ideas for improvement.

Lesson	Author's Approach	Summarizing and Paraphrasing	Critical Thinking
6			
7			
8			
9			
10			

UNIT THREE

Near-Death Experiences

At 1:38 on a Tuesday afternoon, Richard Selzer died. He had lain in a coma for 23 days, and, finally, his heart stopped beating. The doctor and nurses did all they could to get it going again. They gave Selzer electric shocks. They injected medicine right into his chest. But at 1:38 P.M. on April 23, 1991, the doctor declared, "This man is dead." Imagine everyone's surprise when, 10 minutes later, Richard Selzer began breathing again.

Imagine that you have been seriously injured in a car crash. You stop breathing and then rise above your body. Free of pain, you float through a tunnel toward a bright light. But the light fades and you hear someone yell, "This victim is breathing again!" You are one of the millions who have had a Near-Death Experience.

2   No one knows just how Selzer did it. During the minutes he was "dead," he had no heartbeat. He drew no breath. Yet he can describe what went on in the hospital room during those minutes. In 1993 he laid it all out in a book titled *Raising the Dead*.

3   In the book, Selzer details the feeling of being outside his body. Looking down at the hospital bed from above, he could see what was happening. He saw the movements made by nurses after he was declared dead. Just before coming back to life, he heard the beating of wings. Then he felt a veil lifting from his face. That was when he began to breathe again.

4   Richard Selzer is not the only one who has had this kind of brush with death. In a 1982 poll, 8 million Americans reported that they had had Near-Death Experiences, or NDEs. One woman had one when her heart stopped during surgery. Another had one after a bad motorcycle crash. A boy had one when he fell into a washtub and almost drowned.

5   What happens to people during the time they are "dead"? Different people report different things. Still, patterns have formed. Like Richard Selzer, many say they leave their bodies. One person who returned from near death put it this way: "I was out of my body and out of pain. I was up on the ceiling in a corner of the room, looking down, watching doctors and nurses rush around frantically as they worked to save my life." Another said, "I remember just floating up through darkness." Writes David Wheeler, "I felt myself moving away from my physical body. . . . I started to float just a little distance above my body."

6   Next, people often say, they move through a tunnel. They travel toward a bright light. Along the way, they may meet dead relatives. Or they may look back over their whole life. For most people, these moments are pleasant. According to David Wheeler, "I was not frightened. It was a good feeling." Others agree. One woman said, "What I saw while I was dead was so beautiful." Another man claimed his NDE "was the most relaxing and joyful experience of my life."

7   For a few, though, NDEs bring terror. These people feel they are entering a giant void. They see nothing but dark,

empty space. One woman felt she was "falling into a deep well. The fall never seemed to end. I was alone in a strange and unfamiliar world. . . ."

8 People who have had Near-Death Experiences—good or bad—feel their journeys were somehow interrupted. Some say they were pulled back to their bodies. Others say they were sent back against their will. In either case, their hearts resumed beating and they were once again "alive."

9 Are people making up these stories? Perhaps. But it's hard to believe that 8 million folks are lying. So what is going on? Do people really leave their bodies during NDEs? Some scientists say no. They say people may think they are floating. But that feeling is caused by lack of oxygen to the brain. Dr. Bruce Greyson disagrees. Greyson is a college professor. He has spent 20 years studying NDEs. He points out that lack of oxygen causes confusion and panic. NDEs, on the other hand, bring calm, clear thoughts.

10 Could NDEs simply be dreams? Greyson throws out that theory too. Dreams, he says, don't change people's lives. Near-Death Experiences do. NDEs leave people happier and less fearful. After NDEs, people tend to focus on helping others. They may give up high-paying jobs to do work that pays less but is more satisfying.

11 Dr. Sherwin Nuland is not convinced. He thinks NDEs are caused by chemicals in the brain. He says these chemicals are sent out in times of shock. But Nuland can't explain all parts of NDEs. Sometimes, for instance, people pick up information while they float outside their bodies. Greyson tells of a woman who "died" for a short time. While doctors worked to bring her back, Greyson talked with the woman's roommate. Later, the woman could describe that whole conversation. Said Greyson, "Even if she had been conscious, she couldn't possibly have overheard. We were too far away."

12 Sooner or later, we will all find out for ourselves what happens when we die. But people who have had NDEs urge us not to rush things. They enjoyed their contact with death. But they still want to continue their lives here on earth. As Dr. Greyson notes, an NDE does not make someone suicidal. "On the contrary," he says, "it makes life more attractive."

If you have been timed while reading this article, enter your reading time below. Then turn to the Words-per-Minute Table on page 147 and look up your reading speed (words per minute). Enter your reading speed on the graph on page 148.

Reading Time: Lesson 11

_____ : _____
Minutes   Seconds

A | Finding the Main Idea

One statement below expresses the main idea of the article. One statement is too general, or too broad. The other statement explains only part of the article; it is too narrow. Label the statements using the following key:

M—Main Idea   B—Too Broad   N—Too Narrow

_____ 1. Ten minutes after being declared dead, Richard Selzer began to breathe again and later told of his Near-Death Experience.

_____ 2. What people report about their Near-Death Experiences is fascinating.

_____ 3. Sometimes people who seemed to have died come back to life and tell about their Near-Death Experiences.

_____ Score 15 points for a correct M answer.

_____ Score 5 points for each correct B or N answer.

_____ **Total Score:** Finding the Main Idea

B | Recalling Facts

How well do you remember the facts in the article? Put an X in the box next to the answer that correctly completes each statement about the article.

1. One experience that many people report during the time they are "dead" is
   ☐ a. floating out of their bodies.
   ☐ b. falling asleep.
   ☐ c. hearing the sound of the ocean.

2. When Richard Selzer was "dead," he saw
   ☐ a. heaven.
   ☐ b. what was happening near his hospital bed.
   ☐ c. his home and family.

3. In their NDEs, many people report that they meet
   ☐ a. kind strangers.
   ☐ b. angels.
   ☐ c. dead relatives.

4. Some scientists say that the floating feeling that often comes with an NDE is caused by
   ☐ a. panic and fear.
   ☐ b. a lack of oxygen to the brain.
   ☐ c. electrical discharges.

5. Dr. Bruce Greyson believes that NDEs are not simply dreams because
   ☐ a. dreams don't change people's lives.
   ☐ b. people forget dreams.
   ☐ c. many people dream in color.

Score 5 points for each correct answer.

_____ **Total Score:** Recalling Facts

C | Making Inferences

When you combine your own experience with information from a text to draw a conclusion that is not directly stated in that text, you are making an inference. Below are five statements that may or may not be inferences based on information in the article. Label the statements using the following key:

C—Correct Inference   **F—Faulty Inference**

_____ 1. You will probably have a Near-Death Experience at least once in your life.

_____ 2. If many people say the same thing, it must be true.

_____ 3. Reading about others' Near-Death Experiences can make people less afraid of their own deaths.

_____ 4. The only cause of confusion and panic is lack of oxygen to the brain

_____ 5. Someone who has experienced an NDE is likely to be sad and depressed.

_____

Score 5 points for each correct answer.

_____ **Total Score:** Making Inferences

_____

D | Using Words Precisely

Each numbered sentence below contains an underlined word or phrase from the article. Following the sentence are three definitions. One definition is closest to the meaning of the underlined word. One definition is opposite or nearly opposite. Label those two definitions using the following key; do not label the remaining definition.

C—Closest   **O—Opposite or Nearly Opposite**

1. They <u>injected</u> medicine right into his chest.

_____ a. breathed

_____ b. inserted

_____ c. removed

2. I was . . . watching doctors and nurses rush around <u>frantically</u> as they worked to save my life.

_____ a. sadly

_____ b. calmly

_____ c. excitedly

3. For a few, though, NDEs bring <u>terror</u>.

_____ a. intense fear

_____ b. curiosity

_____ c. relaxation

4. People who have had Near-Death Experiences—good or bad— feel their journeys were somehow <u>interrupted</u>.

_____ a. continued

_____ b. stopped

_____ c. misunderstood

5. Greyson throws out that <u>theory</u> too.

_____ a. proven fact

_____ b. study

_____ c. guess

_____ Score 3 points for each correct C answer.

_____ Score 2 points for each correct O answer.

_____ **Total Score:** Using Words Precisely

Enter the four total scores in the spaces below, and add them together to find your Reading Comprehension Score. Then record your score on the graph on page 149.

Score	Question Type	Lesson 11
_____	Finding the Main Idea	
_____	Recalling Facts	
_____	Making Inferences	
_____	Using Words Precisely	
_____	**Reading Comprehension Score**	

Author's Approach

Put an X in the box next to the correct answer.

1. The main purpose of the first paragraph is to

☐ a. suggest that doctors are not careful enough when they declare someone dead.

☐ b. give an example of a situation in which someone came alive again after being declared dead.

☐ c. advertise Richard Selzer's book.

2. What is the authors' purpose in writing "Near-Death Experiences"?

☐ a. to raise the reader's interest in a strange phenomenon

☐ b. to make the reader less afraid of dying

☐ c. to create a spooky mood

3. Judging by statements from the article "Near-Death Experiences," you can conclude that the authors want the reader to think that near-death experiences

☐ a. are simply dreams.

☐ b. can be explained by the action of chemicals in the brain.

☐ c. often change people's lives.

4. In this article, "Greyson is a college professor. He has spent 20 years studying NDEs" means

☐ a. Greyson believes every story about near-death experiences that he hears.

☐ b. Greyson doesn't believe that near-death experiences are at all possible.

☐ c. Greyson takes the idea of near-death experiences very seriously.

_____ Number of correct answers

Record your personal assessment of your work on the Critical Thinking Chart on page 150.

Summarizing and Paraphrasing

Follow the directions provided for questions 1 and 2. Put an X in the box next to the correct answer for question 3.

1. Look for the important ideas and events in paragraphs 7 and 8. Summarize those paragraphs in one or two sentences.

_____

_____

_____

2. Complete the following one-sentence summary of the article using the lettered phrases from the phrase bank below. Write the letters on the lines.

> **Phrase Bank:**
> a. similarities and differences among reported NDEs
> b. Richard Selzer's near-death experience
> c. scientists' attempts to explain NDEs

The article about "Near-Death Experiences" begins with _____, goes on to explain _____, and ends with _____.

3. Read the statement from the article below. Then read the paraphrase of that statement. Choose the reason that best tells why the paraphrase does not say the same thing as the statement.

Statement: After Richard Selzer was declared dead, he felt as if he were outside his body and could see the movements of nurses near his hospital bed.

Paraphrase: Richard Selzer reported that even though everyone thought he was dead, he could still see the nurses move around his bed after his "death."

☐ a. Paraphrase says too much.

☐ b. Paraphrase doesn't say enough.

☐ c. Paraphrase doesn't agree with the statement.

> _____ Number of correct answers
>
> Record your personal assessment of your work on the Critical Thinking Chart on page 150.

Critical Thinking

Put an X in the box next to the correct answer for questions 1, 2, 4, and 5. Follow the directions provided for question 3.

1. Which of the following statements from the article is an opinion rather than a fact?

☐ a. But it's hard to believe that 8 million folks are lying.

☐ b. At 1:38 on a Tuesday afternoon, Richard Selzer died.

☐ c. He points out that lack of oxygen causes confusion and panic.

2. From what the article told about the number of people who have reported near-death experiences, you can predict that

☐ a. soon everyone will have had an NDE.

☐ b. reports of NDEs were just a fad that will soon disappear.

☐ c. people will continue to report NDEs.

3. Choose from the letters below to correctly complete the following statement. Write the letters on the lines.

On the positive side, _____, but on the negative side _____.

   a. only a very sick or injured person can experience an NDE

   b. NDEs are usually described as joyful experiences

   c. about 8 million people have reported NDEs

4. According to scientists, what is the cause of the feeling of floating reported by people who have had NDEs?

☐ a. chemical reactions in the brain

☐ b. lack of oxygen

☐ c. insanity

5. What did you have to do to answer question 1?

☐ a. find an opinion (what someone thinks about something)

☐ b. find a cause (why something happened)

☐ c. find a comparison (how things are the same)

_____ Number of correct answers

Record your personal assessment of your work on the Critical Thinking Chart on page 150.

Personal Response

A question I would like answered by Richard Selzer is:

_____

_____

_____

Self-Assessment

One good question about this article that was not asked would be

_____

_____

_____

And the answer is _____

_____

_____

_____

Is Anyone Out There?

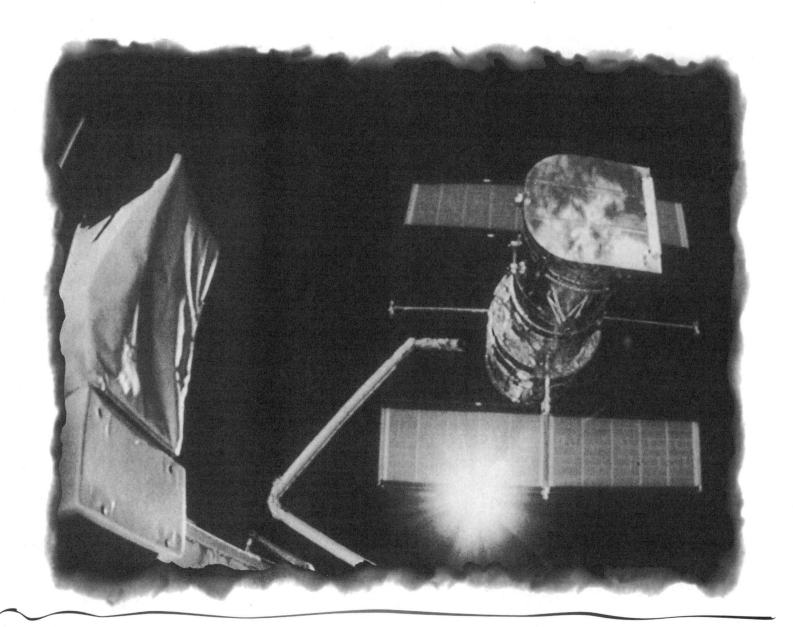

Is there intelligent life elsewhere in the universe? Some people would answer that question with a loud "Yes!" In fact, some people would say that space travelers from other worlds visit us all the time. As proof, these people would point to UFOs (Unidentified Flying Objects). There are thousands of UFO sightings every year. Believers say UFOs are really spaceships from other planets. So for UFO fans, there is no question. They

Even the Hubble Space Telescope shown here cannot focus on anything so small as a planet around a distant star. Still, many scientists believe that there are many planets in the universe that can support life. Will creatures from those planets ever contact us? Are they trying to contact us now?

are sure someone else is "out there" and, in fact, is watching us all the time.

2   Yet despite all the sightings, most scientists do not believe in UFOs. There are a couple of reasons for this. For one thing, how would creatures from some other planet know about us? We have been sending radio signals to outer space for only a few years. These signals have not had time to reach any distant planets. Our nearest neighbors may be hundreds of light-years away. (A light-year measures how far light travels in one year. The speed of light is 186,000 miles per second.) So if we do have neighbors, they won't get our radio signals for years to come.

3   Some people think aliens could have noticed us even without radio signals. If that's the case, they say, couldn't these aliens drop by for a visit from time to time? It's not likely. Certainly humans have not figured out a way to whiz from one solar system to another. Again, it's a distance problem. The nearest star is more than four light-years away. It would take our best spaceship 100,000 years to get there! And most stars are much, much farther away.

4   So if aliens were going to visit us, they'd have to be a lot smarter than we are. They would have to figure out how to fly close to the speed of light. Some distant civilization might have the skills to do that. But, again, most scientists doubt it. Besides, suppose that some life form is that advanced. Why would these creatures want to visit Earth? Compared to them, humans would seem pretty simple-minded. So if aliens were going to zip off to some other planet, chances are it wouldn't be ours.

5   Given all this, it seems safe to conclude that UFOs are not for real. Little green people in flying saucers are probably not flashing through the sky every year to check us out. Does that mean that there is no intelligent life anywhere else in the universe? Not at all! Most scientists believe there is lots of intelligent life out there. Just look at the facts. In our galaxy alone—the Milky Way—there are about 400 billion stars. There is a strong chance that many of these stars have planets that can support life. Scientists have made a rough guess about how many. They figure that there may be as many as 10,000

civilizations in the Milky Way. Now consider that there are at least 400 billion galaxies! Surely these other galaxies also contain planets that could support life.

6   It's frustrating to think that we might never see the life forms that inhabit other planets. But couldn't we at least talk to them? Scientists say that is possible. It could be done using radio waves. These waves travel at the speed of light. Even here, though, there are some problems. Imagine radio signals coming from a planet that is 10,000 light-years away. By the time we get these signals, the creatures who sent them might no longer exist. After all, it would have taken the signals 10,000 years to reach Earth. A lot can happen in that time. Think about our own civilization. Will the human race be here 10,000 years from now? Or will some disease have killed us all? Will we have wiped ourselves out with wars or pollution? No one knows the answer. In fact, there are no guarantees we'll last even another hundred years. So by the time creatures on another planet receive our radio signals, we might be long gone.

7   There's one more thing to keep in mind. The life that exists on another planet might not look anything at all like human life. Scientists urge us to stop thinking in terms of "little green men." In truth, we have no idea what other forms of intelligent life would look like. Like us, they would most likely be made up of atoms and molecules. But beyond that, it's anyone's guess. They could be as different from us as we are from alligators. Also, the idea of flying saucers is ours, not theirs. If aliens did visit us, their technology would be far beyond ours. It would be beyond anything we could imagine. As scientist Carl Sagan has said, it would look to us as if the creatures were performing "magic."

If you have been timed while reading this article, enter your reading time below. Then turn to the Words-per-Minute Table on page 147 and look up your reading speed (words per minute). Enter your reading speed on the graph on page 148.

Reading Time: Lesson 12

———— : ————
Minutes   *Seconds*

A | Finding the Main Idea

One statement below expresses the main idea of the article. One statement is too general, or too broad. The other statement explains only part of the article; it is too narrow. Label the statements using the following key:

M—Main Idea   B—Too Broad   N—Too Narrow

_____ 1. Travel to the nearest star would take our space ships 100,000 years.

_____ 2. Many people believe in intelligent life on other planets.

_____ 3. Although intelligent life may exist on other planets, you are not likely, for a variety of reasons, to meet an alien here on Earth.

_____ Score 15 points for a correct M answer.

_____ Score 5 points for each correct B or N answer.

_____ **Total Score:** Finding the Main Idea

B | Recalling Facts

How well do you remember the facts in the article? Put an X in the box next to the answer that correctly completes each statement about the article.

1. People on Earth have been sending radio signals into outer space for
   ☐ a. only a few years.
   ☐ b. centuries.
   ☐ c. most of human history.

2. Scientists believe there may be intelligent life on other planets because
   ☐ a. they have received messages from aliens.
   ☐ b. there may be many planets similar to ours.
   ☐ c. the planets are so far away.

3. Radio waves travel
   ☐ a. slower than the speed of light.
   ☐ b. faster than the speed of light.
   ☐ c. at the speed of light.

4. Intelligent life from other planets would probably
   ☐ a. look just like humans.
   ☐ b. be made up of atoms and molecules.
   ☐ c. look like alligators.

5. If aliens were advanced enough to travel to Earth, they would probably think that humans were
   ☐ a. not as intelligent as they were.
   ☐ b. more intelligent than they were.
   ☐ c. just as intelligent as they were.

Score 5 points for each correct answer.

_____ **Total Score:** Recalling Facts

C Making Inferences

When you combine your own experience with information from a text to draw a conclusion that is not directly stated in that text, you are making an inference. Below are five statements that may or may not be inferences based on information in the article. Label the statements using the following key:

C—Correct Inference   F—Faulty Inference

_____ 1. The major reason for human efforts to make contact with other intelligent life is human curiosity.

_____ 2. If alien life forms ever come to Earth, their most likely reason will be to destroy us, their rivals.

_____ 3. As scientists discover more stars, more of them expect that other stars' planets will have the right conditions for intelligent life.

_____ 4. If friendly aliens ever visit Earth, we could apply much of their medical knowledge to ourselves.

_____ 5. Unless other intelligent beings can translate the languages used in our radio broadcasts, they will never realize that Earth has intelligent life.

Score 5 points for each correct answer.

_____ **Total Score:** Making Inferences

D Using Words Precisely

Each numbered sentence below contains an underlined word or phrase from the article. Following the sentence are three definitions. One definition is closest to the meaning of the underlined word. One definition is opposite or nearly opposite. Label those two definitions using the following key; do not label the remaining definition.

C—Closest   O—Opposite or Nearly Opposite

1. As proof, these people would point to UFOs (Unidentified Flying Objects).

_____ a. powerful

_____ b. not recognized

_____ c. known

2. These signals have not had time to reach any distant planets.

_____ a. far away

_____ b. strange

_____ c. close

3. Besides, suppose that some life form is that advanced.

_____ a. curious

_____ b. behind the times

_____ c. ahead of our time

4. It's frustrating to think that we might never see the life forms that inhabit other planets.

_____ a. soothing

_____ b. annoying

_____ c. funny

5. By the time we get these signals, the creatures who sent them might no longer <u>exist</u>.

_____ a. listen

_____ b. live

_____ c. die out

```
_____ Score 3 points for each correct C answer.

_____ Score 2 points for each correct O answer.

_____ Total Score: Using Words Precisely
```

Enter the four total scores in the spaces below, and add them together to find your Reading Comprehension Score. Then record your score on the graph on page 149.

Score	Question Type	Lesson 12
_____	Finding the Main Idea	
_____	Recalling Facts	
_____	Making Inferences	
_____	Using Words Precisely	
_____	**Reading Comprehension Score**	

Author's Approach

Put an X in the box next to the correct answer.

1. The authors use the first sentence of the article to

☐ a. inform the reader of the main question the article will try to answer.

☐ b. compare humans and other life forms.

☐ c. entertain the reader with a joke.

2. What do the authors mean by the statement "Compared to them [life forms so advanced they could travel at nearly the speed of light], humans would seem pretty simple-minded"?

☐ a. Humans would look very attractive to advanced life forms.

☐ b. To advanced life forms, humans would not seem intelligent enough to be at all interesting.

☐ c. Advanced life forms would be fascinated by humans.

3. Some people believe that humans will soon talk to creatures on other planets using radio waves. Choose the statement below that best explains how the authors address the opposing point of view in the article.

☐ a. Creatures who could send out radio waves would have to be more advanced than humans and would not be interested in communicating with humans.

☐ b. Scientists on Earth only started sending out radio signals a few years ago.

☐ c. By the time a radio wave message reached Earth from a distant planet, those who sent it might no longer exist, so they could not talk back.

```
_____ Number of correct answers

Record your personal assessment of your work on the
Critical Thinking Chart on page 150.
```

Summarizing and Paraphrasing

Follow the directions provided for question 1. Put an X in the box next to the correct answer for the other questions.

1. Reread paragraph 2 in the article. Below, write a summary of the paragraph in no more than 25 words.

_____

_____

_____

_____

Reread your summary and decide whether it covers the important ideas in the paragraph. Next, decide how to shorten the summary to 15 words or less without leaving out any essential information. Write this summary below.

_____

_____

_____

2. Read the statement from the article below. Then read the paraphrase of that statement. Choose the reason that best tells why the paraphrase does not say the same thing as the statement.

Statement: Like humans, creatures from other planets would be made up of atoms and molecules.

Paraphrase: Although they would be made up of atoms and molecules like humans, space creatures may not look like us.

☐ a. Paraphrase says too much.

☐ b. Paraphrase doesn't say enough.

☐ c. Paraphrase doesn't agree with the statement.

3. Choose the best one-sentence paraphrase for the following sentence from the article: "They [scientists] figure that there may be as many as 10,000 civilizations in the Milky Way."

☐ a. The Milky Way has been proven to be home to at least 10,000 civilizations.

☐ b. In the Milky Way alone, scientists guess that as many as 10,000 civilizations may exist.

☐ c. Scientists believe that at least 10,000 planets in the Milky Way have civilizations.

_____ Number of correct answers

Record your personal assessment of your work on the Critical Thinking Chart on page 150.

Critical Thinking

Put an X in the box next to the correct answer for questions 1, 2, and 4. Follow the directions provided for the other questions.

1. Which of the following statements from the article is an opinion rather than a fact?

☐ a. The nearest star is more than four light-years away.

☐ b. It's frustrating to think that we might never see the life forms that inhabit other planets.

☐ c. A light-year measures how far light travels in one year.

2. From the information in paragraph 7, you can predict that if an alien life form landed on Earth,

☐ a. it would look exactly like humans.

☐ b. humans would recognize it immediately.

☐ c. humans might not notice it.

3. Choose from the letters below to correctly complete the following statement. Write the letters on the lines.

According to the article, _____ would cause humans to _____, and the effect would be that _____.

a. humans would think the creatures were performing magic

b. be amazed

c. the advanced technology of aliens who visited Earth

4. How is "Is Anyone Out There?" related to *Weird Science*?

☐ a. This article is a humorous look at an interesting question.

☐ b. This article shows that some people believe in things that are not possible.

☐ c. This article discusses a question that can best be answered by using scientific reasoning.

5. In which paragraph did you find your information or details to answer question 3? _____

_____ Number of correct answers

Record your personal assessment of your work on the Critical Thinking Chart on page 150.

Personal Response

I can't believe _____

_____

_____

_____

Self-Assessment

A word or phrase in the article that I do not understand is _____

_____

_____

_____

It's All in Your Head

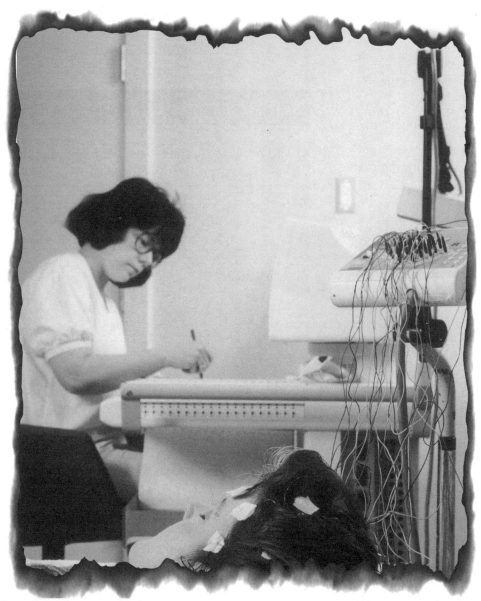

"You are what you eat." Have you ever been told that as you pop potato chips into your mouth? Actually, it's a pretty fair warning. Your body turns the food you eat into blood, bones, and muscles. Eat bad food and you will probably end up with a weak body. Eat good food and you will probably end up with a strong body.

2   Everyone agrees that eating healthy foods will help make a healthy body. But now scientists are also discovering

Through modern technology, researchers can attach special wires to patients' skin to find out what's happening inside. The wires pick up data about patients' involuntary actions, such as heartbeat and nerve impulses. Then, using the information, patients learn how to control some of these actions.

that "you are what you think." That doesn't mean you can think your way into the Olympics. And it doesn't mean that you can close your eyes and heal a broken leg. But your thoughts, or brain waves, can do some remarkable things. They can cure headaches. They can help lower blood pressure. Your thoughts can even direct messages to certain nerve cells in your body. This ability can restore the use of muscles lost through an accident or disease.

3   This new form of mind control is called *biofeedback*. In truth, it isn't really new. People in Asia have been using biofeedback for centuries. In the United States, however, use of biofeedback is new. It began during the 1960s. Some young people began studying the religions of Asia. They learned about biofeedback and began to practice it. These people used it to help them meditate, or focus their thinking. At first, western scientists laughed at biofeedback. They thought it was just a fad. Slowly, however, the practice took hold. One study after another showed that it really worked. Maybe, scientists thought, biofeedback wasn't so crazy after all.

4   Clearly, your brain can control certain things. For example, it can command your legs to run. It can direct your hand to write a letter. And it can tell your mouth to speak. Those are called *voluntary* actions. You make up your mind to do something. But your body does other things that are very hard to control. How, for instance, can you control your heartbeat? Or the circulation of your blood? Or your body's temperature? Those bodily functions are called *involuntary*. They just happen. You have no control over them . . . or do you? The goal of biofeedback is to help you control those involuntary actions.

5   Here is how it works. You sit in a chair in front of a TV monitor. Special wires are taped to your head, neck, back, and fingers. The wires can detect tiny changes in your body's involuntary actions. The other ends of the wires are hooked up to a biofeedback machine. Let's say that you are trying to reduce your heart rate. Soft music begins to play. You try to relax. You might try deep breathing, or you might concentrate on thinking pleasant thoughts. You might imagine yourself lying on the beach in the warm sun.

The machine measures your heart rate and "feeds back" information about how well you are doing.

6   You can see your progress on the TV screen. A line or a series of beeps records your heart rate. By watching that line, you can learn what thoughts slow down your heart. You might find that an image of a sunny beach lowers your heart rate. But imagining that same beach bathed in moonlight does not. Slowly, you learn how to reduce your heart rate. Once this is done, you no longer need the machine. You have learned to control your body's "involuntary" actions.

7   But biofeedback can work even greater wonders. Since the 1970s, it has been used to help epileptics control seizures. These seizures cause epileptics to shake without control. Sometimes they faint. These attacks are caused by electrical discharges in the brain.

8   Using biofeedback, many epileptics have learned to control their seizures. They discover what feelings or situations trigger seizures. They learn to avoid those feelings. In a sense, then, biofeedback shows epileptics how to "rewire" their brains.

9   Biofeedback can even help badly hurt people. In the 1980s, a car accident left Tammy DeMichael with a broken neck and a crushed spinal cord. She had no feeling in her arms or legs. Traditional medicine did nothing to help her. It looked as if she would have to spend the rest of her life in a wheelchair. Luckily, she still had a few good nerves reaching her arm muscles. They were not enough to let DeMichael move her arm, but they gave her some hope.

10   Could her brain be taught to use those remaining nerves? Bernard Brucker, her doctor, thought so. He hooked DeMichael up to a biofeedback machine. The TV monitor showed a blue line. That line represented impulses moving from her brain through her spine to her arm muscles. DeMichael concentrated as hard as she could. Slowly, she got the line on the TV screen to move up. Still, her arm didn't move. But the line showed that more impulses were reaching her arm. One day, DeMichael got the arm to move. Everyone in the room cheered. She did the same thing with her legs. It took several years, but biofeedback worked. DeMichael learned to walk using just a cane.

11   Western scientists no longer scoff at biofeedback. They see it as a hot new medical tool. It has been used to teach some children how to pay better attention in school. Astronauts use it to fight motion sickness during space travel. It has even been used to treat certain forms of cancer. Clearly, biofeedback is here to stay. Bernard Brucker put it this way. "Biofeedback," he says, "has opened up a whole new era in human learning."

A Finding the Main Idea

One statement below expresses the main idea of the article. One statement is too general, or too broad. The other statement explains only part of the article; it is too narrow. Label the statements using the following key:

M—Main Idea   **B—Too Broad**   **N—Too Narrow**

_____ 1. Until a few years ago, biofeedback was not taken seriously by Western scientists.

_____ 2. Biofeedback is helping more people take control of their bodies.

_____ 3. Scientists are eager to find new ways to treat diseases and other physical problems.

_____ Score 15 points for a correct M answer.

_____ Score 5 points for each correct B or N answer.

_____ **Total Score:** Finding the Main Idea

B Recalling Facts

How well do you remember the facts in the article? Put an X in the box next to the answer that correctly completes each statement about the article.

1. When Western scientists first heard about biofeedback, they thought it
   ☐ a. was just a fad.
   ☐ b. was useful only for young people.
   ☐ c. made a lot of sense.

2. Body actions that are hard to control are called
   ☐ a. electrical.
   ☐ b. voluntary.
   ☐ c. involuntary.

3. In biofeedback, wires attached to your body
   ☐ a. control body functions.
   ☐ b. detect tiny changes.
   ☐ c. give you small electrical charges.

4. A car accident left Tammy DeMichael with
   ☐ a. no sense of balance.
   ☐ b. a broken neck and a crushed spinal cord.
   ☐ c. no arms or legs.

5. Epileptic seizures are caused by
   ☐ a. electrical discharges in the brain.
   ☐ b. improper diet.
   ☐ c. too many chemicals in the brain.

Score 5 points for each correct answer.

_____ **Total Score:** Recalling Facts

C Making Inferences

When you combine your own experience with information from a text to draw a conclusion that is not directly stated in that text, you are making an inference. Below are five statements that may or may not be inferences based on information in the article. Label the statements using the following key:

C—Correct Inference   F—Faulty Inference

_____ 1. Soon, diseases will be wiped out by biofeedback.

_____ 2. Some Asian religions make use of the methods that are part of biofeedback.

_____ 3. If you are always upset and nervous, your body systems will be affected.

_____ 4. In most cases, biofeedback works better than medicine.

_____ 5. Western scientists never trust any methods of health care that come from religion.

Score 5 points for each correct answer.

_____ **Total Score:** Making Inferences

D Using Words Precisely

Each numbered sentence below contains an underlined word or phrase from the article. Following the sentence are three definitions. One definition is closest to the meaning of the underlined word. One definition is opposite or nearly opposite. Label those two definitions using the following key; do not label the remaining definition.

C—Closest   O—Opposite or Nearly Opposite

1. But your thoughts, or brain waves, can do some <u>remarkable</u> things.

_____ a. amazing

_____ b. nice

_____ c. normal

2. The wires can <u>detect</u> tiny changes in your body's involuntary actions.

_____ a. ignore

_____ b. cause

_____ c. discover

3. Slowly, you learn how to <u>reduce</u> your heart rate.

_____ a. increase

_____ b. lower

_____ c. pay attention to

4. Your thoughts can even <u>restore</u> the use of muscles lost through an accident or disease.

_____ a. put back in working order

_____ b. damage

_____ c. display

5. Western scientists no longer <u>scoff at</u> biofeedback.

_____ a. honor

_____ b. make fun of

_____ c. point to

_____ Score 3 points for each correct C answer.

_____ Score 2 points for each correct O answer.

_____ **Total Score:** Using Words Precisely

Enter the four total scores in the spaces below, and add them together to find your Reading Comprehension Score. Then record your score on the graph on page 149.

Score	Question Type	Lesson 13
_____	Finding the Main Idea	
_____	Recalling Facts	
_____	Making Inferences	
_____	Using Words Precisely	
_____	**Reading Comprehension Score**	

Author's Approach

Put an X in the box next to the correct answer.

1. What do the authors mean by the statement "You are what you eat"?

☐ a. Your thoughts influence your diet.

☐ b. Different kinds of people should eat different kinds of foods.

☐ c. A person's diet makes a difference in his or her health.

2. Which of the following statements from the article best describes an involuntary action?

☐ a. to write a letter

☐ b. the circulation of your blood

☐ c. to speak

3. From the statements below, choose those that you believe the authors would agree with.

☐ a. Biofeedback takes a great deal of concentration.

☐ b. Electrical discharges in the brain have nothing to do with emotions.

☐ c. Biofeedback holds great promise as a medical treatment.

4. The authors probably wrote this article to

☐ a. inform readers of a promising new medical tool.

☐ b. prove to readers that biofeedback will work for them.

☐ c. persuade doctors to have all their patients try biofeedback.

_____ Number of correct answers

Record your personal assessment of your work on the Critical Thinking Chart on page 150.

Summarizing and Paraphrasing

Follow the directions provided for questions 1 and 2. Put an X in the box next to the correct answer for question 3.

1. Look for the important ideas and events in paragraphs 7 and 8. Summarize those paragraphs in one or two sentences.

_____

_____

_____

2. Reread paragraph 4 in the article. Below, write a summary of the paragraph in no more than 25 words.

_____

_____

_____

_____

Reread your summary and decide whether it covers the important ideas in the paragraph. Next, decide how to shorten the summary to 15 words or less without leaving out any essential information. Write this summary below.

_____

_____

3. Choose the sentence that correctly restates the following sentence from the article: "Western scientists no longer scoff at biofeedback."

☐ a. Western science has no place for biofeedback.

☐ b. Western scientists no longer believe in biofeedback.

☐ c. Western scientists are now taking biofeedback more seriously.

_____ Number of correct answers

Record your personal assessment of your work on the Critical Thinking Chart on page 150.

Critical Thinking

Follow the directions provided for questions 1 and 3. Put an X in the box next to the correct answer for the other questions.

1. For each statement below, write *O* if it expresses an opinion or write *F* if it expresses a fact.

_____ a. Involuntary actions include regulating the heartbeat, controlling blood circulation, and maintaining body temperature.

_____ b. Thinking about a day at the beach is sure to lower your heart rate.

_____ c. Tammy DeMichael suffered a broken neck and a crushed spinal cord in a car accident.

2. From the article, you can predict that if you were blind,

☐ a. biofeedback machines as described in this article would not work for you.

☐ b. your doctor would probably suggest that you try biofeedback machines to regain your sight.

☐ c. you would not need biofeedback machines.

3. Choose from the letters below to correctly complete the following statement. Write the letters on the lines.

According to the article, _____ cause _____, and the effect is that epileptics have _____.

a. unpleasant emotions

b. seizures

c. electrical discharges in the brain

4. What did you have to do to answer question 2?

☐ a. find an opinion (what someone thinks about something)

☐ b. find a description (how something looks)

☐ c. make a prediction (what might happen next)

_____ Number of correct answers

Record your personal assessment of your work on the Critical Thinking Chart on page 150.

Personal Response

I agree with the author because _____

_____

_____

_____

_____

Self-Assessment

When reading the article, I was having trouble with _____

_____

_____

_____

_____

Cryonics: Death on Ice

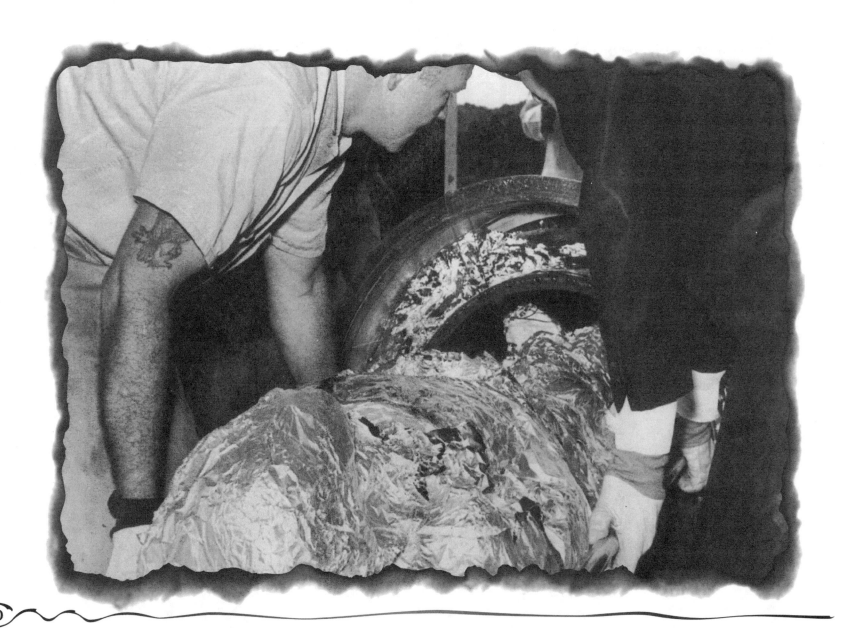

Like most people, Dick Clair wanted to live a long life. He didn't quite make it, however. At the age of 57, he grew ill and died. But Clair, a TV comedy writer, was determined to have the last laugh. So he arranged to have his body frozen instead of buried in the ground. Someday, Clair hoped, scientists would find a cure for the disease that killed him. Then doctors could thaw out his body and cure him. Once revived, Clair could start writing TV comedy shows again.

In the future, whatever disease killed this person being placed in a metal tube may be curable. So he or she has been frozen, using a practice called cryonics. When a cure for the disease is found, the person's body may be thawed out, giving him or her a second chance at life.

2 Like a growing number of people, Clair believed in cryonics. *Cryonics* is the practice of freezing a body at the moment of death. Cryonic suspension was first done in 1968. Since then, many people have been frozen. Hundreds more have signed up for future freezing. Some even plan to have their favorite dog or cat frozen with them. That way, owner and pet may be reunited when a cure is found.

3 Cryonics takes careful planning. As soon as someone dies, oxygen must be pumped into the body. That keeps the body tissues from decaying. The body must also be packed in ice to keep it cool. Then the blood is drained and replaced with a special fluid. Next, the body is wrapped in plastic and zipped into a sleeping bag. Finally, the bag is put into a nine-foot metal tube. A special cooling gas, called liquid nitrogen, is pumped into the tube. Slowly, the temperature drops all the way to –321°F. At such a super-low temperature, a body will last almost forever. The decay that would take one second at room temperature would take 30 trillion years at –321°F! So people such as Clair can be kept on ice for a very long time.

4 Cyronics is not a proven science. There are still plenty of bugs to be worked out. One of the biggest hurdles is the freezing process itself. Parts of a human body can be preserved for a short time. A heart, for example, can be saved for several hours. This has made human heart transplants possible. But saving a *whole body* for a long time is much harder.

5 Freezing will preserve it. But freezing also tends to destroy it. The human body is made up of cells surrounded by water. As soon as the temperature drops below 32°F, that water starts to expand. It forms ice crystals. That causes tearing and damages body tissue. All bodies in cryonic suspension have suffered tissue damage. There is no guarantee that scientists will ever figure out a way to repair the damage.

6 Let's assume, however, that they do. Let's also assume that scientists solve all the other technical problems. Moral questions would still remain. Who should get frozen? Cryonic suspension is not cheap. At present, it costs more than $100,000. Some people opt for a cheaper solution. They pay $35,000 each to have just their heads frozen.

They are gambling that scientists will someday be able to attach each head to a brand new body. Still, freezing any part of the body takes big bucks. Does that mean only rich people should get a second chance at life?

7   Surely, not everyone can be frozen. The world already has too many people. What would happen if lots of "dead" people came back to life? The world could not support them all. So someone would have to decide who gets frozen and who doesn't.

8   Should the young be favored over the old? Should law-abiding people be picked over criminals? Would a musician be selected ahead of a street sweeper?

9   There are other problems as well. Let's suppose a wife dies and is cryonically suspended. Is her widower free to remarry? What happens to her money and property? If she is thawed out, can she move back into her old house? Can she demand her old job back? How would she talk to her kids if she's now 20 or 30 years *younger* than they are? Suppose she doesn't come back for a thousand years. What would she do in this strange new world? How would she make a living? Who would be her friends?

10   The questions go on and on. Still, people cling to the hope that they can someday live again. In 1993 *Omni* magazine held an essay contest. The winner got a free cryonic suspension. *Omni* received hundreds of essays. People gave lots of good reasons for wanting to live again. Some wrote that they were excited about the distant future and wanted to see it for themselves. Others wanted to carry knowledge of today's world to the people of the future. Still others felt that they had missed out on things in this life and wanted a second chance. One young reader—the winner—had been injured in a car accident. He wanted to come back "healthy and healed."

11   Cryonics may prove to be a false hope. All the frozen dead bodies may be just that—frozen and dead. But cryonics brings hope to those who believe in it. Even if it doesn't work out, what have they lost besides the money? As Dick Clair once said, "To me, [cryonics] is a way to stay alive."

If you have been timed while reading this article, enter your reading time below. Then turn to the Words-per-Minute Table on page 147 and look up your reading speed (words per minute). Enter your reading speed on the graph on page 148.

Reading Time: Lesson 14

_____ : _____
Minutes   *Seconds*

A Finding the Main Idea

One statement below expresses the main idea of the article. One statement is too general, or too broad. The other statement explains only part of the article; it is too narrow. Label the statements using the following key:

M—Main Idea   B—Too Broad   N—Too Narrow

_____ 1. Cryonics is the art of freezing a body at the moment of death.

_____ 2. Some people are paying $35,000 to have just their heads frozen after death.

_____ 3. Cryonics offers hope for renewed life, but also poses problems that have not yet been worked out.

_____ Score 15 points for a correct M answer.

_____ Score 5 points for each correct B or N answer.

_____ **Total Score:** Finding the Main Idea

B Recalling Facts

How well do you remember the facts in the article? Put an X in the box next to the answer that correctly completes each statement about the article.

1. Cryonics suspension was first done in
   ☐ a. 1995.
   ☐ b. 1968.
   ☐ c. 1924.

2. A body ready to be frozen is put into a metal tube, which is then filled with
   ☐ a. oxygen.
   ☐ b. ice.
   ☐ c. liquid nitrogen.

3. When the temperature drops below 32°F, water starts to
   ☐ a. expand.
   ☐ b. shrink.
   ☐ c. boil.

4. Ice crystals in body cells cause
   ☐ a. tissue damage.
   ☐ b. the body to stop aging.
   ☐ c. moral problems.

5. Bodies kept at −321°F will resist decay
   ☐ a. for about 50 years.
   ☐ b. for about 1,000 years.
   ☐ c. almost forever.

Score 5 points for each correct answer.

_____ **Total Score:** Recalling Facts

C Making Inferences

When you combine your own experience with information from a text to draw a conclusion that is not directly stated in that text, you are making an inference. Below are five statements that may or may not be inferences based on information in the article. Label the statements using the following key:

C—Correct Inference   F—Faulty Inference

_____ 1. People who spend their money on cryonic suspension have faith in the future.

_____ 2. Most people who have undergone cryonic suspension were wealthy when they were alive.

_____ 3. Someday there will be a worldwide organization that will decide who will be frozen.

_____ 4. If the temperature of bodies that are frozen rises too high, the bodies will begin to decay.

_____ 5. Most people who die from now on will have their bodies frozen so they can live again later.

Score 5 points for each correct answer.

_____ **Total Score:** Making Inferences

D Using Words Precisely

Each numbered sentence below contains an underlined word or phrase from the article. Following the sentence are three definitions. One definition is closest to the meaning of the underlined word. One definition is opposite or nearly opposite. Label those two definitions using the following key; do not label the remaining definition.

C—Closest   O—Opposite or Nearly Opposite

1. Once <u>revived</u>, Clair could start writing TV comedy shows again.

_____ a. restored to life

_____ b. frozen

_____ c. put to death

2. That way, owner and pet may be <u>reunited</u> when a cure is found.

_____ a. remembered

_____ b. brought back together

_____ c. separated again

3. One of the biggest <u>hurdles</u> is the freezing process itself.

_____ a. signals

_____ b. helps

_____ c. obstacles

4. The <u>decay</u> that would take one second at room temperature would take 30 trillion years at −321°F!

_____ a. building up of the body

_____ b. breakdown of the body

_____ c. change in the body

5. That causes tearing and <u>damages</u> body tissues.

_____ a. improves

_____ b. affects

_____ c. harms

_____ Score 3 points for each correct C answer.

_____ Score 2 points for each correct O answer.

_____ **Total Score:** Using Words Precisely

Enter the four total scores in the spaces below, and add them together to find your Reading Comprehension Score. Then record your score on the graph on page 149.

Score	Question Type	Lesson 14
_____	Finding the Main Idea	
_____	Recalling Facts	
_____	Making Inferences	
_____	Using Words Precisely	
_____	**Reading Comprehension Score**	

Author's Approach

Put an X in the box next to the correct answer.

1. The main purpose of the first paragraph is to

☐ a. explain exactly how cryonic suspension is done.

☐ b. make fun of the idea of cryonically suspending anyone.

☐ c. give an example of one person who was cryonically suspended.

2. What is the authors' purpose in writing "Cryonics: Death on Ice"?

☐ a. to encourage readers to have their bodies frozen after death

☐ b. to inform readers about a way of preserving a body after death

☐ c. to emphasize the similarities between cryonic suspension and mummification

3. Many people think that cryonic suspension is a wonderful idea. Choose the statement below that best explains how the authors address the opposing point of view in the article.

☐ a. The author points out that cryonic suspension may cause legal problems for the person who returns to life many years after "death."

☐ b. The author points out that cryonic suspension must happen quickly after the moment of death.

☐ c. The authors point out that cryonic suspension may give some people a second chance at life.

_____ Number of correct answers

Record your personal assessment of your work on the Critical Thinking Chart on page 150.

Summarizing and Paraphrasing

Follow the directions provided for the following questions.

1. Complete the following one-sentence summary of the article using the lettered phrases from the phrase bank below. Write the letters on the lines.

Phrase Bank:

a. how cryonic suspension is done

b. legal and moral questions about cryonic suspension and reasons why some people want to try it

c. a discussion about how popular cryonic suspension has become

The article "Cryonics: Death on Ice" begins with _____, goes on to explain _____, and ends with _____.

2. Reread paragraph 5 in the article. Below, write a summary of the paragraph in no more than 25 words.

_____

_____

_____

_____

Reread your summary and decide whether it covers the important ideas in the paragraph. Next, decide how to shorten the summary to 15 words or less without leaving out any essential information. Write this summary below.

_____

_____

_____

_____ Number of correct answers

Record your personal assessment of your work on the Critical Thinking Chart on page 150.

Critical Thinking

Follow the directions provided for questions 1 and 3. Put an X in the box next to the correct answer for the other questions.

1. For each statement below, write *O* if it expresses an opinion or write *F* if it expresses a fact.

_____ a. The temperature of a body that is surrounded by liquid nitrogen slowly drops to −321°F.

_____ b. Cryonic suspension is a fascinating idea.

_____ c. Cryonic suspension is too dangerous and should be stopped.

2. From the information in paragraph 9, you can predict that

☐ a. when the first person who has been cryonically suspended awakes, he or she will have plenty of problems to work out.

☐ b. before the first person who has been cryonically suspended awakes, all the problems will have been worked out.

☐ c. no one whose wife or husband has been cryonically suspended will ever remarry.

3. Choose from the letters below to correctly complete the following statement. Write the letters on the lines.

On the positive side, _____, but on the negative side, _____.

   a. cryonic freezing takes careful planning

   b. the cryonically suspended person may have a chance to live again

   c. when he or she awakes, the cryonically suspended person may have trouble fitting into the world

4. How is cryonic suspension related to *Weird Science*?

☐ a. Cryonic suspension may not work.

☐ b. Cryonic suspension is nontraditional and is not accepted by many scientists.

☐ c. Cryonic suspension has become quite popular but it raises many problems.

5. What did you have to do to answer question 3?

☐ a. find a contrast (how things are different)

☐ b. find an opinion (what someone thinks about something)

☐ c. find a cause (why something happened)

_____ Number of correct answers

Record your personal assessment of your work on the Critical Thinking Chart on page 150.

Personal Response

If I were the authors, I would add _____

_____

because _____

_____

Self-Assessment

Which concepts or ideas from the article were difficult to understand?

_____

_____

Which were easy?

_____

_____

Needles That Cure

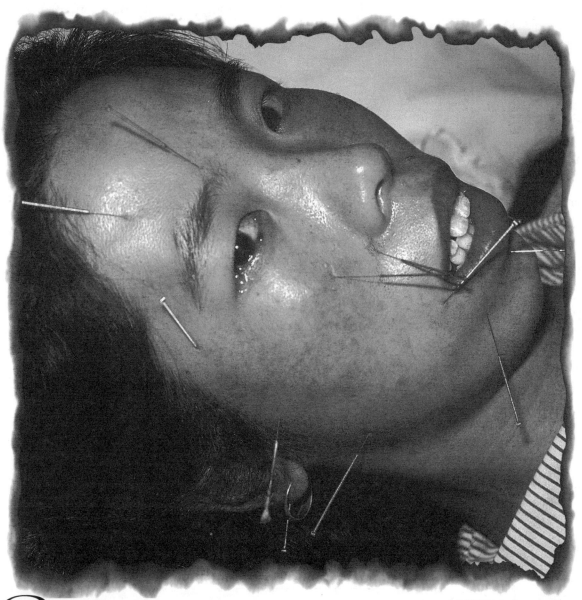

Everyone knows that feet are good for walking, running, and kicking a soccer ball. But did you know that your feet can also play a role in curing headaches, stomachaches, and toothaches? Some people say you can get rid of these and many other ailments just by jabbing a needle into your foot.

2   It sounds crazy at first. But according to the ancient art of acupuncture, it works. A needle stuck into a specific point on your second toe can banish

Could well-placed needles stuck in your body cause your aches and pains to disappear? Those who practice an ancient Chinese treatment called acupuncture believe that is true.

headaches. A needle between your second and third toe can rid you of a sore throat. A needle put into the outside of your foot can stimulate your vision.

3   Acupuncture began in China more than four thousand years ago. It is based on the belief that there is a natural flow of energy inside each human being. This energy, or life force, is called *qi* (pronounced CHEE). The qi is said to flow along certain pathways in the body. These pathways, called meridians, are like rivers. When they flow freely, you feel strong and healthy. But if one of your meridians gets blocked, the flow of energy is disrupted. Your qi becomes unbalanced. Too much qi builds up in one part of your body. Other parts don't get enough. That's where the needles come in. By inserting needles in just the right spots, you can unblock your meridians and get your qi flowing correctly again.

4   No one has ever been able to prove the existence of these energy pathways. But over the years Chinese practitioners have fine-tuned their view of qi. They have identified 14 meridians. They have named about 1,500 points on the body

where these meridians can get clogged. And they have figured out which points need to be opened to relieve different pains. Let's say your immune system is weak. In that case you'll need a needle put in near your elbow. But if nausea is your problem, the needle must go lower down on your arm, right near your wrist.

5   When people in Europe and America first heard about acupuncture, they were skeptical. For a long time they paid no attention to stories about it. But by the 1970s some doctors were taking a closer look. Some of them began to experiment with it. What they found surprised them. Many patients said that acupuncture lessened their pain. When nothing else would work, it often gave them relief.

6   One woman was suffering from asthma. Her doctor gave her medicine, but it made her body swell up like a balloon. Soon she weighed 300 pounds. Still, the asthma attacks kept coming. As soon as she started acupuncture treatment, though, the asthma went away. The woman lost 80 pounds and was able to throw away all her asthma medicine.

7   Another patient had neck pain that she could not shake. After a year of

misery, she turned to acupuncture. "All of a sudden, the pain was gone," she said.

8   Does this mean that the Chinese view of energy pathways is accurate? Maybe not. Western doctors have another theory about why acupuncture works. They have found that sticking needles into the body can stimulate the nervous system. The

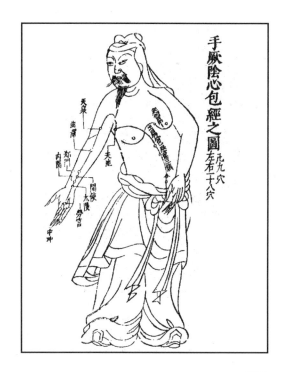

nervous system then releases chemicals into your body. Many doctors think it is these chemicals that take away the pain.

9   Some people have said that acupuncture is all in your head. That is, it only works because you expect it to work. But that would not explain why it works on animals. Cows, dogs, cats, and horses have all been helped by acupuncture. And certainly these animals were not true believers!

10   Acupuncture has also worked on many humans who didn't think it would. One such patient was Zang-Hee Cho. Cho was a California physicist. In 1993 he fell while hiking on a mountain. He hurt his back so badly he could barely walk. Some of his relatives said he should try acupuncture, but he scoffed at the idea. He didn't think there was anything to it. When he finally agreed to give it a try, he was amazed. "After about 10 minutes I felt the pain melting away," he said.

11   Cho later set up a study to find out how acupuncture affects the brain. He watched needles being put into patients' feet. The goal was to unclog the qi that flowed to the eyes. That sounded like nonsense to Cho. But then he took pictures of the patients' brains during the procedure. He was shocked. Their brains showed the same activity as when a light was shone in their eyes. "I never thought anything would happen," Cho said. "But it's very clear that stimulating the acupuncture point triggers activity in the visual cortex [part of the brain]."

12   Other studies have found that acupuncture increases the flow of blood to the brain. It sends more blood to the part of the brain that registers pain. Thanks to studies like these, more and more people are lining up for treatment. The World Health Organization has even drawn up a list of ailments that can be treated this way. The list has everything from chest infections to earaches to back pain.

13   If you should ever try acupuncture, here's what you will find. Up to 20 or more needles will be stuck into various parts of your body. These needles are very thin, and most patients say they don't cause much pain. Some of the needles may not be pushed in very far. But others may be put as deep as three inches. The needles will stay in place for 15 to 30 minutes. Practitioners say you might feel relief right away or you might need several sessions to feel better.

14   One word of warning: In most states, acupuncturists don't need medical degrees. So if you think your qi is out of line, be careful. Pick someone who knows what he or she is doing. A bad acupuncturist could damage your nerves or puncture your lung. If that were to happen, you'd be in worse shape than you were when you started.

If you have been timed while reading this article, enter your reading time below. Then turn to the Words-per-Minute Table on page 147 and look up your reading speed (words per minute). Enter your reading speed on the graph on page 148.

Reading Time: Lesson 15

_____ : _____
Minutes   *Seconds*

A Finding the Main Idea

One statement below expresses the main idea of the article. One statement is too general, or too broad. The other statement explains only part of the article; it is too narrow. Label the statements using the following key:

M—Main Idea   B—Too Broad   N—Too Narrow

_____ 1. Acupuncture is based upon the idea that there is a flow of energy called qi inside every human being. Pain and disease result when a person's qi becomes blocked.

_____ 2. Acupuncture is an ancient Chinese practice for relieving pain and disease by sticking needles into specific points in a person's body.

_____ 3. Although some medical treatments have been around for centuries, scientists have only now begun studying them.

_____ Score 15 points for a correct M answer.

_____ Score 5 points for each correct B or N answer.

_____ **Total Score:** Finding the Main Idea

B Recalling Facts

How well do you remember the facts in the article? Put an X in the box next to the answer that correctly completes each statement about the article.

1. Acupuncture probably started in China about
   ☐ a. 400 years ago.
   ☐ b. 4,000 years ago.
   ☐ c. 10,000 years ago.

2. The term *qi* refers to
   ☐ a. people trained to do acupuncture.
   ☐ b. the method of sticking needles at particular body points.
   ☐ c. the energy, or life force, in every person.

3. Some Western doctors think that acupuncture makes some patients feel better because
   ☐ a. it has magical powers.
   ☐ b. it causes the nervous system to release pain-killing chemicals.
   ☐ c. the practitioners of acupuncture hypnotize the patients.

4. A California physicist named Zang-Hee Cho turned to acupuncture after he
   ☐ a. fell while hiking on a mountain.
   ☐ b. was injured in a car crash.
   ☐ c. developed severe asthma.

5. Once the needles are inserted into a patient's body, they usually stay there
   ☐ a. overnight.
   ☐ b. for only a few seconds.
   ☐ c. for 15 to 30 minutes.

Score 5 points for each correct answer.

_____ **Total Score:** Recalling Facts

C | Making Inferences

When you combine your own experience with information from a text to draw a conclusion that is not directly stated in that text, you are making an inference. Below are five statements that may or may not be inferences based on information in the article. Label the statements using the following key:

C—Correct Inference   **F—Faulty Inference**

_____ 1. Western doctors have always been anxious to adopt the medical practices of other cultures.

_____ 2. People in pain are willing to take chances with almost any treatment that promises relief.

_____ 3. There is much that Western doctors don't know about how the human body works.

_____ 4. Chinese doctors are just as suspicious of Western medicine as Western doctors are suspicious of acupuncture.

_____ 5. Chinese people don't use any medical treatments besides acupuncture.

Score 5 points for each correct answer.

_____ **Total Score:** Making Inferences

D | Using Words Precisely

Each numbered sentence below contains an underlined word or phrase from the article. Following the sentence are three definitions. One definition is closest to the meaning of the underlined word. One definition is opposite or nearly opposite. Label those two definitions using the following key; do not label the remaining definition.

C—Closest   **O—Opposite or Nearly Opposite**

1. A needle stuck into a specific point on your second toe can <u>banish</u> headaches.

_____ a. drive away

_____ b. resemble

_____ c. cause

2. A needle put into the outside of your foot can <u>stimulate</u> your vision.

_____ a. deaden

_____ b. excite

_____ c. replace

3. But if one of your meridians gets blocked, the flow of energy is <u>disrupted</u>.

_____ a. amazing

_____ b. calmed

_____ c. disturbed or upset

4. They have named about 1,500 points on the body where these meridians can get <u>clogged</u>.

_____ a. broken

_____ b. blocked

_____ c. flowing freely; open

5. After a year of <u>misery</u>, she turned to acupuncture.

_____ a. pleasure

_____ b. effort

_____ c. suffering

_____ Score 3 points for each correct C answer.

_____ Score 2 points for each correct O answer.

_____ **Total Score:** Using Words Precisely

Enter the four total scores in the spaces below, and add them together to find your Reading Comprehension Score. Then record your score on the graph on page 149.

Score	Question Type	Lesson 15
_____	Finding the Main Idea	
_____	Recalling Facts	
_____	Making Inferences	
_____	Using Words Precisely	
_____	**Reading Comprehension Score**	

Author's Approach

Put an X in the box next to the correct answer.

1. What do the authors mean by the statement "These pathways, called meridians, are like rivers"?

☐ a. Meridians allow qi to flow just as rivers allow water to flow.

☐ b. Meridians carry qi and water around the body.

☐ c. Meridians carry chemicals around the body just as rivers carry boats.

2. Some people say that acupuncture only seems to work because the patients want it to work. Choose the statement below that best explains how the authors address the opposing point of view in the article.

☐ a. The authors note that acupuncture has also helped animals, who could not have simply believed in it.

☐ b. The authors note that it is often the people who are most desperate who find relief in acupuncture.

☐ c. The authors point out that many people are surprised that acupuncture works so well.

3. The authors probably wrote this article to

☐ a. ridicule those who believe in acupuncture.

☐ b. inform readers about a promising medical treatment.

☐ c. encourage everyone to try acupuncture.

_____ Number of correct answers

Record your personal assessment of your work on the Critical Thinking Chart on page 150.

Summarizing and Paraphrasing

Put an X in the box next to the correct answer for questions 1 and 3. Follow the directions provided for question 2.

1. Below are summaries of the article. Choose the summary that says all the most important things about the article but in the fewest words.

   ☐ a. The human body has a life force that needs to flow around the body freely. When the life force is blocked, pain and disease may result. The practice of acupuncture allows the body energy to flow where it needs to go.

   ☐ b. If you should decide to try acupuncture, be aware that there are risks associated with it. In the hands of someone who is not skillful, the needles inserted into your body may actually caused damage instead of relief.

   ☐ c. Acupuncture, an ancient Chinese medical treatment to relieve pain, involves inserting needles at strategic points throughout the body. Many patients report that acupuncture gives relief from pain when Western medicines have failed. Although Western doctors rejected acupuncture at first, they have recently begun to study it.

2. Reread paragraph 5 in the article. Below, write a summary of the paragraph in no more than 25 words.

   _____

   _____

   _____

   _____

Reread your summary and decide whether it covers the important ideas in the paragraph. Next, decide how to shorten the summary to 15 words or less without leaving out any essential information. Write this summary below.

_____

_____

_____

3. Choose the sentence that correctly restates the following sentence from the article: "Thanks to studies like these, more and more people are lining up for [acupuncture] treatment."

   ☐ a. Those who practice acupuncture are thanking scientists who made the studies because more people are asking for treatments.

   ☐ b. More people are choosing to try acupuncture because of these studies.

   ☐ c. The acupuncture practitioners are gratefully lining up to be part of these studies.

   _____ Number of correct answers

   Record your personal assessment of your work on the Critical Thinking Chart on page 150.

Critical Thinking

Follow the directions provided for questions 1, 3, and 5. Put an X in the box next to the correct answer for the other questions.

1. For each statement below, write *O* if it expresses an opinion or write *F* if it expresses a fact.

   _____ a. Qi is just a figment of desperate people's imaginations.

   _____ b. Acupuncture is the best treatment for people who suffer pain.

   _____ c. Chinese practitioners of acupuncture have identified about 1,500 points where meridians can get clogged.

2. From the article, you can predict that if Western scientists continue to study acupuncture, they will

   ☐ a. decide to stop using Western medicine and use only acupuncture to relieve pain.

   ☐ b. eventually discover what makes acupuncture work.

   ☐ c. decide that acupuncture doesn't really work for anyone.

3. Choose from the letters below to correctly complete the following statement. Write the letters on the lines.

   In the article, _____ and _____ are different.

   a. Zang-Hee Cho's early opinion about acupuncture

   b. most Western doctors' early opinion about acupuncture

   c. Chinese practitioners' opinion about acupuncture

4. According to some Western doctors, what is the effect of inserting needles into the body?

   ☐ a. The qi is allowed to flow freely through the meridians.

   ☐ b. The nervous system sends chemicals into the body.

   ☐ c. Clogged blood vessels are cleaned out.

5. In which paragraph did you find your information or details to answer question 4? _____

_____ Number of correct answers

Record your personal assessment of your work on the Critical Thinking Chart on page 150.

Personal Response

Would you recommend this article to other students? Explain.

_____

_____

_____

Self-Assessment

I can't really understand how _____

_____

_____

_____

Compare and Contrast

Think about the articles you have read in Unit Three. Pick three subjects you want to learn more about. Write the titles of the articles that tell about them in the first column of the chart below. Use information you learned from the articles to fill in the empty boxes in the chart.

Title	What facts or ideas had you known before reading the article?	Which ideas from the article were new to you?	Which ideas made you curious to learn more?

The subject I am most interested in learning more about is _____. The three best places to do research on this subject are

_____

_____

Words-per-Minute Table

Unit Three

Directions: If you were timed while reading an article, refer to the Reading Time you recorded in the box at the end of the article. Use this Words-per-Minute Table to determine your reading speed for that article. Then plot your reading speed on the graph on page 148.

Lesson	11	12	13	14	15	
No. of Words	854	800	930	865	1,006	
Minutes and Seconds						*Seconds*
1:30	563	533	620	577	671	**90**
1:40	512	480	558	519	604	**100**
1:50	466	436	507	472	549	**110**
2:00	427	400	465	433	503	**120**
2:10	394	369	429	399	464	**130**
2:20	366	343	399	371	431	**140**
2:30	342	320	372	346	402	**150**
2:40	320	300	349	324	377	**160**
2:50	301	282	328	305	355	**170**
3:00	285	267	310	288	335	**180**
3:10	270	253	294	273	318	**190**
3:20	256	240	279	260	302	**200**
3:30	244	229	266	247	287	**210**
3:40	233	218	254	236	274	**220**
3:50	223	209	243	226	262	**230**
4:00	214	200	233	216	252	**240**
4:10	205	192	223	208	241	**250**
4:20	197	185	215	200	232	**260**
4:30	190	178	207	192	224	**270**
4:40	183	171	199	185	216	**280**
4:50	177	166	192	179	208	**290**
5:00	171	160	186	173	201	**300**
5:10	165	155	180	167	195	**310**
5:20	160	150	174	162	189	**320**
5:30	155	145	169	157	183	**330**
5:40	151	141	164	153	178	**340**
5:50	146	137	159	148	172	**350**
6:00	142	133	155	144	168	**360**
6:10	138	130	151	140	163	**370**
6:20	135	126	147	137	159	**380**
6:30	131	123	143	133	155	**390**
6:40	128	120	140	130	151	**400**
6:50	125	117	136	127	147	**410**
7:00	122	114	133	124	144	**420**
7:10	119	112	130	121	140	**430**
7:20	116	109	127	118	137	**440**
7:30	114	107	124	115	134	**450**
7:40	111	104	121	113	131	**460**
7:50	109	102	119	110	128	**470**
8:00	107	100	116	108	126	**480**

Plotting Your Progress: Reading Speed

Unit Three

Directions: If you were timed while reading an article, write your words-per-minute rate for that article in the box under the number of the lesson. Then plot your reading speed on the graph by putting a small X on the line directly above the number of the lesson, across from the number of words per minute you read. As you mark your speed for each lesson, graph your progress by drawing a line to connect the X's.

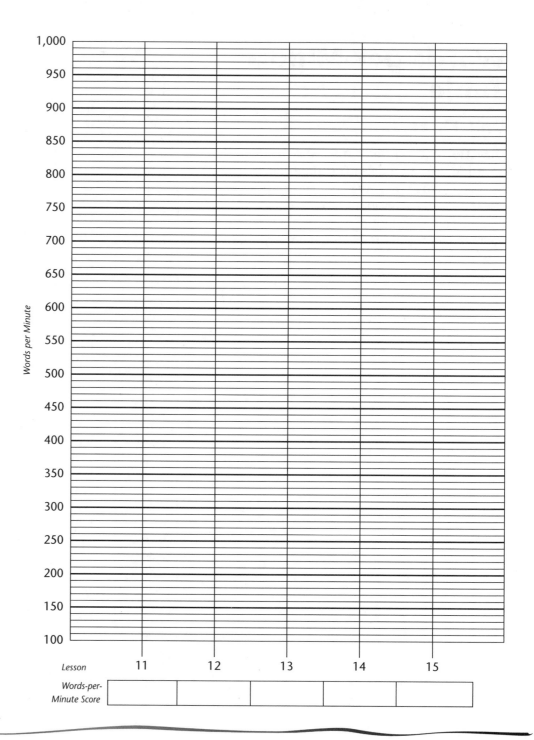

Lesson	11	12	13	14	15
Words-per-Minute Score					

Plotting Your Progress: Reading Comprehension

Unit Three

Directions: Write your Reading Comprehension Score for each lesson in the box under the number of the lesson. Then plot your score on the graph by putting a small X on the line directly above the number of the lesson and across from the score you earned. As you mark your score for each lesson, graph your progress by drawing a line to connect the X's.

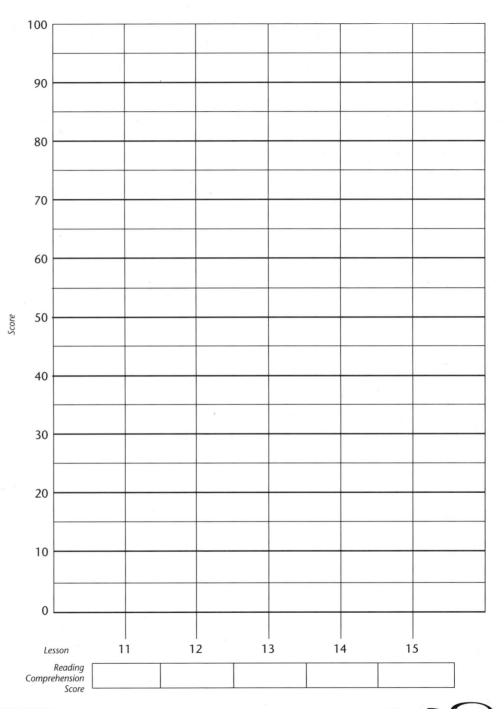

Lesson	11	12	13	14	15
Reading Comprehension Score					

Plotting Your Progress: Critical Thinking

Unit Three

Directions: Work with your teacher to evaluate your responses to the Critical Thinking questions for each lesson. Then fill in the appropriate spaces in the chart below. For each lesson and each type of Critical Thinking question, do the following: Mark a minus sign (–) in the box to indicate areas in which you feel you could improve. Mark a plus sign (+) to indicate areas in which you feel you did well. Mark a minus-slash-plus sign (–/+) to indicate areas in which you had mixed success. Then write any comments you have about your performance, including ideas for improvement.

Lesson	Author's Approach	Summarizing and Paraphrasing	Critical Thinking
11			
12			
13			
14			
15			

Photo Credits